ORNAMENTAL GRASS GARDENING

ORNAMENTAL GRASS GARDENING

DESIGN IDEAS, FUNCTIONS AND EFFECTS

BY THOMAS A. REINHARDT, MARTINA REINHARDT AND MARK MOSKOWITZ

Photography by Derek Fell

Macdonald Orbis

A MACDONALD ORBIS BOOK

Copyright © 1989 by Michael Friedman Publishing Group, Inc.

Published in Great Britain in 1989 by Macdonald & Co. (Publishers) Ltd.
London & Sydney

A member of Maxwell Perganon Publishing Corporation plc.

Reinhardt, Thomas
Ornamental grass gardening.
1. Gardens. Ornamental grasses.
I. Title.   II. Reinhardt, Martina.   III. Moscowitz, Mark.
635.9'349

ISBN 0-356-17514-6

ORNAMENTAL GRASS GARDENING: Design Ideas, Functions, and Effects
was prepared and produced by
Michael Friedman Publishing Group, Inc.
15 West 26th Street
New York, New York 10010

Editor: Tim Frew
Designer: Devorah Levinrad
Art Director: Mary Moriarty
Photo Editor: Christopher Bain
Production Manager: Karen L. Greenberg

Typeset by BPE Graphics, Inc.
Colour separations by South Sea International Press
Printed and bound in Hong Kong by Leefung-Asco Printers Ltd.

Macdonald & Co. (Publishers) Ltd.
Greater London House
Hampstead Road
London NW1 7QX

Dedication

We'd like to dedicate this book to all the many friends, teachers, students, colleagues, and supporters, who have given us strength and energy on our journeys of garden creation. They are the soil from which this seed has grown.

Acknowledgments

We'd like to thank all those who have helped bring about this book. First and foremost we'd like to thank Esty Kishon Moskowitz. Her creative inspiration, her contribution to the design section, her assistance in preparing the manuscript, all were essential ingredients. To our many teachers both in the universities we have attended and in the many gardens from which we have learned. Especially to the Professors at Wein Stephan West Germany, who enriched us with their knowledge and gave us the opportunity to study and work in the Stauden Sichtungs garden. To our students who helped research the information contained in the dictionary of grasses, and to our many colleagues in the U.S. and abroad who have contributed many valuable insights into gardening with grasses. We hope this book will be able to add something to their knowledge or at least to their library. Finally, we would like to credit much of what might be taken for original contributions to the work of the great grass specialist Karl Foerster. May his work soon be published in English.

TABLE OF CONTENTS

Introduction
page 8

*O*ne   *Understanding Grasses*
page 10

*T*wo   *The Basics of Ornamental Grass Gardening*
page 24

TABLE OF CONTENTS

Three — Designing with Ornamental Grasses
page 44

Four — A Catalogue of Grasses
page 88

Appendix
page 118

Sources, Bibliography, & Index
page 122

Introduction

Grasses—they grow in lawns and by the seaside, are found in thick forests and bogs, and along highways and vast prairies. They have played a major role in the ecology of plant life and in the development of human society. Many basic crops—wheat, rice, and corn—are grasses. Today, grasses are playing an increasing role in the garden landscape. The versatility, adaptability, and exquisite beauty of ornamental grasses makes them the perfect companions and counterpoint plants to flowering perennials and woody ornamentals. Some grasses work well as ground covers, others serve better as accent pieces or focal points.

This book explores the many uses of ornamental grasses to the garden designer and shows how they can enrich and beautify the landscape, provide new aesthetic dimensions, and extend the seasonal duration of the garden.

With their vast array of colours—from blue to fiery red—and their varied shapes and sizes—from dense, ground-level clumps to towering 20-foot- (6-metre-) tall reeds—ornamental grasses are valued for their beauty and durability in landscape borders, beds, and gardens. Unlike lawn grasses, ornamentals are left to flourish in their natural state. Lawn grasses are frequently cut, and are, in fact, invigorated by the process. Ornamental grasses, on the other hand, are weakened and eventually perish through frequent low cuttings. Unlike lawns, whose beauty lies in the form and texture of a carpeted expanse, ornamental grasses are valued for their individual aesthetic properties, even when planted en masse. Some are pendulous; some stand erect. They form mounds or have vertical culms (stems), are single-coloured or variegated, grow singularly from one clump or from spreading rhizomes (a horizontal stem on or under the ground that sends up a succession of stems or leaves at the apex). In these ways, ornamental grasses give a sense of texture, form, and colour. Taller-growing species cast dominant silhouettes that act as accent points, while lower-growing species act as contrasting ground covers. Indeed, there are limitless possibilities when designing with ornamental grasses. One can build an interesting and aesthetically commanding picture that contains both horizontal and vertical elements, distinctness and mass, regular and irregular textures and colours, natural forms, and calculated design concepts.

In addition to being aesthetically appealing, ornamental grasses require very little maintenance. They usually do not require deadheading, staking, or spraying, and most grasses grow in a variety of environmental conditions and continue to be visually appealing throughout the year.

Despite the adaptability and versatility of ornamental grasses, many people do not think of using them in their landscaping concept. In fact, most nonexperts do not even know what is a grass and what is not. This book takes a look at the differences and similarities of the three families primarily used in ornamental grass gardening—the Gramineae family (grasses), the Cyperaceae family (sedges), and the Juncaceae family (rushes). It then goes on to show how and where these "grasses" can be effectively incorporated into a well-planned landscape design. Whether used as specimens, ground covers, borders, or accents, ornamental grasses offer a wide range of possibilities to enhance the beauty of a garden year-round.

Understanding Grasses

W hat is a grass? This sounds like a simple question, but, unfortunately, it has no simple answer. Many of the plants used in ornamental grass gardens are not really grasses at all, but members of the grasslike families of rushes and sedges. The first section of this chapter deals with the technical botanical terminology and distinctions relevant to the subject of grasses. We feel this is useful information to anyone interested in the particulars of grasses and ornamental grass gardening. The next few sections look at the various roles of grasses in the environment and in the development of society.

One of the basic misconceptions about grasses is that all plants that are grasslike are members of the grass family. In the strict botanical sense the grass family is called Gramineae. But any book that is written for the garden designer and amateur gardener cannot stop short of including other popular grasslike families—the two most important of which are the Juncaceae family (rushes) and the Cyperaceae family (sedges). In this book we will refer to members of the Gramineae family as grasses, and to rushes and sedges as grasslike.

Pennisetum alopecuroides (Australian Fountain Grass), far left, is known for its spikelike, plumy panicles which appear in the late summer or early autumn and stay attractive until winter. Although members of the *Carex* species, near left, have many grasslike characteristics, they are actually members of the Cyperaceae family.

The Gramineae Family

The Gramineae family includes lawn grasses, bamboo, cereals (such as wheat and rice), and ornamentals such as Fescue (*Festuca*), Chinese Silver Grass (*Miscanthus*), Red Switch Grass (*Panicum*), and Fountain Grass (*Pennisetum*). It is a very large family made up of about 620 genera and 9000 species of perennial and annual grasses found worldwide. Members of the Gramineae family are distinguished from other families by certain characteristics in their foliage, inflorescence, seeds, and fruits. Members of grasslike families may share one or two of these characteristics, but not all three.

When most people think of grass they think of the plant's leaves—the most recognizable characteristic of the grass plant. All grasses have parallel veins running through the long narrow blades of their foliage. This foliage can either stand erect or be pendulant, and can be either flexible or rigid.

Secondly and more distinctly, grasses are known by their inflorescence—the way in which a group of flowers or bracts (scale-like leaves) is arranged on one main stem. In grasses, the inflorescence is composed of both flowers and subtended bracts. (Subtended means that the bracts stand below the flower.) The bract/flower components that make up a grass's inflorescence are called spikelets. These spikelets are usually green, yellow, brown, or silver-grey—rarely having bright colours—and are either sessile (without a stem) or pediceled (with a stem). In addition, Gramineae spikelets develop in three different arrangements:

(1) Spike—This is an unbranched, elongated inflorescence, in which the flowers are sessile.
(2) Raceme—This is an unbranched, elongated inflorescence in which the flowers are pediceled.
(3) Panicle—This arrangement has inflorescences that are branched. These branches, in turn, are either racemes (above) or corymbs, which are flat-topped, short, and broad inflorescence.

The third basic characteristic of the Gramineae pertains to the fruit and seeds. The fruit is called the caryopsis, a term used almost exclusively in relation to grasses. A caryopsis consists of the seed and an adherent fruit wall which is sometimes enclosed by the palea (inner bract) and the lemma (the outer bract). The caryopsis is dry and indehiscent (meaning the fruit does not open spontaneously when ripe). The ovary (the ovule-bearing or seed-carrying part of the fruit) is

classified as superior, meaning that it is located above the perianth (the floral envelope). In addition, the stamen (the pollen-bearing organ) and the pericarp (the wall of the ovary) are attached to the seed.

Here it is important to point out that other grasslike families have capsules or nuts rather than caryopses. This is why Nut Grass (*Cyperus hydra*) is actually a sedge rather than a grass. But many grasslike families share with the grasses their monocotyledonous nature. This means that when the seeds of these plants germinate, they show only one leaf—called the seed leaf, or cotyledon. This is contrary to many plants that are dicotyledonous, where two seed leaves show when the plant is germinating.

*T*he inflorescence is one of the most distinctive characteristics of members of the Gramineae family. It consists of bract/flower combinations called spikelets, which develop in either a spike, raceme, or panicle arrangement.

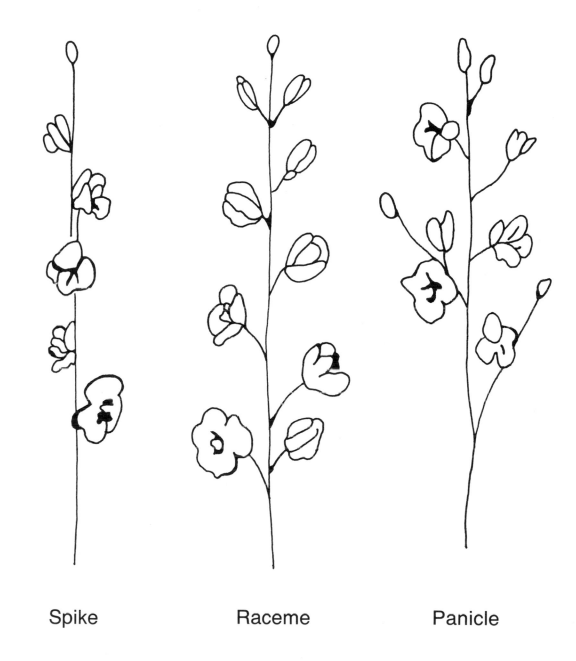

Spike   Raceme   Panicle

Rushes (Juncaceae)

Rushes are a relatively small family, comprising only eight or nine genera that share common characteristics in their leaves, flowers, and fruit. First, unlike grasses, rushes have sepals. These are the leaves or leaflike parts of the flower's calyx, or husk.

Secondly, the leaves of the rushes have a cylindrical shape, are pliant, and carry small, greenish bisexual flowers. These flowers carry three to six stamens, and a superior ovary (as with the Gramineae). The ovaries are either single-celled or three-celled. If the ovaries are three-celled, the placentas (a zone of tissue to which the ovules are attached) are arranged axially (located near the centre of a compound ovary). If the ovaries are single-celled, the placentas are arranged parietally (found on the ovule wall).

Perhaps the greatest difference between rushes and grasses has to do with the fruit. The fruit of rushes is a three-celled capsule (a dry, dehiscent fruit) composed of two or more united carpels (units composing the ovary).

Although they are botanically different, many grasslike plants have similar visual characteristics to grass. Palm Branch Sedges, left, look like grasses; however, they are actually members of the Cyperaceae family.

Sedges (Cyperaceae)

The sedge family is composed of about eighty genera of mostly perennial herbs.

The stems of sedges are solid, unlike members of the Gramineae family, whose stems are hollow except at the swollen nodes. Still, the stems of sedges are similar enough to those of Gramineae for both to be termed culms, a term reserved for the stems of only these two families. However, unlike grasses, the culms of sedges are mostly three-angled. The mode of arrangement of the inflorescence consists of one or more spikelets that are subtended by one or more involucre bracts (close spirals of small leaves). The small flowers carry one or three stamens and a superior, one-celled ovary. The fruit is an achene with a three-angled convex shape, a characteristic exclusive to sedges.

As we have seen, these three families have both important similarities and important differences. Although botanically distinct, they have enough similar visual characteristics to cause much confusion, leading many designers to treat them as similar elements. The confusion is also one of language. For example, Rush Wheat (*Triticum junceum*) is not a rush but a grass; Nut Grass (*Cyperus esculentus*) is not a grass but a sedge. And bulrushes are not rushes—they're either *Typha latifolia* (Typhaceae, the cattail family) or *Scirpus lacustris* (the sedge family). Even the Bible differs in terminology from our modern botanical classification for the bulrushes. In Exodus 2:3, in the passage "She took for him [the babe Moses] an arke of bulrushes," "bulrushes" refers to papyrus, which is a sedge.

In a discussion of ornamental grass gardening, it is important to include rushes and sedges along with grasses, because they are all so closely identified. Even botanically knowledgeable nurserymen commonly catalogue grasses into a three-category typology. But although most people closely associate these two grasslike families with grasses themselves, the reader should not be led to conclude that rushes and sedges are the only grasslike families. Arrow grass is not a grass but a grasslike bog genera, *Triglochin*, a member of the Juncaginaceae family. Both *Acorus*, of the Arum family, and certain irises, such as *Iris cristata*, are grasslike in appearance.

The three basic families of plants we will continue to concern ourselves with are a loosely associated set, determined more by popular opinions and tradition than by pure botanical foundations.

*D*une grass helps control erosion from wind and water along the seaside; while, on mountains and hillsides grasses produce much-needed humus that helps the soil retain nutrients and moisture.

Grasses in Their Natural Habitat

More often than not, grasses and grasslike families are the first plants to settle in a new environment, preparing the way for the other plants that follow. They do this pioneer work in three basic, but very important, ways. When grasses go dormant after the growing season, the yearly growth dies and is converted to humus, which supplies nutrients and helps the soil absorb water. Secondly, and even more importantly, grasses and grasslike families serve to control erosion. Along riverbanks, in bogs, on dunes, and on steep mountain slopes, grasses help hold the soil in place. Finally, grasses serve to catch and retain water, making the moisture available for other plants.

As a result of their pioneer role, grasses are found in a wide range of climatic and ecological conditions. They are usually hardy and adaptable, growing well in environments where other plants cannot survive. For example, grasses thrive in areas flooded by stormy seas, in the floodplains of

*B*ecause of their hardy disposition, grasses have served a pioneer role in nature—making the soil and habitat more suitable for other plants. *Elymus* (European Beach Grass), right, is an effective erosion control both in the wild and in the garden.

rivers and lakes, on salt marshes and saltwater beaches, on arid, sunny southern slopes, on the edges of forests and under the forest canopy, and on mountains up to the snow line.

Many grasses cope through a division of labour. This enables them to cooperate in establishing a more suitable ecosystem. For example, deep-rooting species loosen the soil with their roots and at the same time prevent erosion. Grasses that have a lot of top growth bring about humus production, and grasses that are ground covers retain soil moisture and also serve as erosion controls.

MOUNTAIN GRASSES

Mountain grasses are the largest category of grasses—primarily because the wide degree of environmental conditions found in the mountains have caused a wide range of evolutionary adaptations. In fact, most of the grain grasses commonly associated with the prairie are related to the wild mountain grasses

The mountains of Middle Asia and Ethiopia brought about the most important wild grasses from which the grains originated. The largest variety of grasses developed in the mountain valleys and mountain tundras of northern Iran, and in the Pamir Mountains—areas largely untouched by glacial activ-

ity. Along with development of grain came the development of man as a city dweller. Dense populations in these areas eventually brought about mass migration, the beginning of agricultural cultivation, and the spreading of grains to new regions.

AGRICULTURAL GRASSES

There are three main types of agricultural grasses. Food grasses (i.e. cereals), forage grasses (which are grown for hay, pasturage, and silage), and soil-holding grasses used as sand binders or to fix steep banks with their strong, creeping rhizomes (runners). Without these three types of grasses, it would be difficult to imagine the development of human civilization.

RIVER, LAKE, AND POND GRASSES

As is the case with the mountain grasses, the grasses, rushes, and sedges found by riverbanks, lakes, and ponds help establish the ecosystem of which they are a part. Grasses such as *Phragmites australis*—located the world over—secure the health of the water and the life cycle of animals. In fact, the greatest value of reeds is their stabilizing influence on wetlands throughout the world.

WOODLAND GRASSES

Another ecosystem where grasses play an important role is the woodlands. Woodland grasses are able to cope with dense shade and heavy root competition. These grasses are so hardy that in some cases they survive for several decades. Woodland grasses serve as a hiding place for small animals, provide food for larger animals, and are a much-needed source of humus. *Carex*, found the world over, is one of the

most important and well-known woodland grasslike genera. (It is a sedge) *Carex pendula* (common sedge grass) is found throughout Western Europe; *Carex morrowii* and *Carex conica* are located in Japan; and *Carex grayi* and *Carex plantaginea* are native to the eastern part of the United States. *Carex* makes an ideal addition to a woodland garden. It can be planted in shady locations as bed edgings and as accent plants in rock gardens.

*A*lthough not always thought of as a grass by the layman, wheat, the world's most important agricultural grass, is a member of the Gramineae family.

Grasses and Society

Through the use of grasses, man has moved from nomad to farmer. Grasses in the form of grains revolutionized human society, enabling man to start settlements with permanent foundations. Grass products brought about new forms of social interaction, trade, and storage, and were used to feed livestock as well as people. Corn, wheat, millet, rice, oats, and barley are all grasses. Without the cultivation and harvesting of grasses, man would not have had sugarcane—once the primary source of sugar.

Grasses have also served man in ways indirectly linked to food. Papyrus, the ancient writing paper of Egypt and the Near East, was made from pressing together thin strips of wet pith (the soft, spongy central cylinder of the stem of the papyrus plant). *Juncus effusus* (Soft Rush), the most important member of the *Juncus* genera, is a major source of matting and is grown in Japan for weaving tatami, the traditional mat of the Japanese home.

No discussion of grasses, rushes, and sedges that serve man could ever exclude bamboo (Gramineae family). Bamboo has been used to make fences, fishing rods, water pipes, and housing materials; and the shoots make quite a tasty dish. In the garden, bamboo is used as screens, ground covers, accent pieces, and specimens. The bamboos are so important that they have their own subfamily or tribe, called *Bambuseae*. Though mainly native to Asia, some of the species of *Arundinaria* and *Bambusa* are native to the Western Hemisphiere. Bamboo ranges from the tree-size, timber-producing species (species of *Bambusa* and *Dendrocalamus*) to shrubs (species of *Arundinaria*, *Bambusa*, *Chimonobambusa*, *Phyllostachys*, *Pseudosasa*, *Sasa*, and *Sinarundinaria*) and ground-cover-size plants (species of *Arundinaria*, *Sasa*, and *Shibateae*).

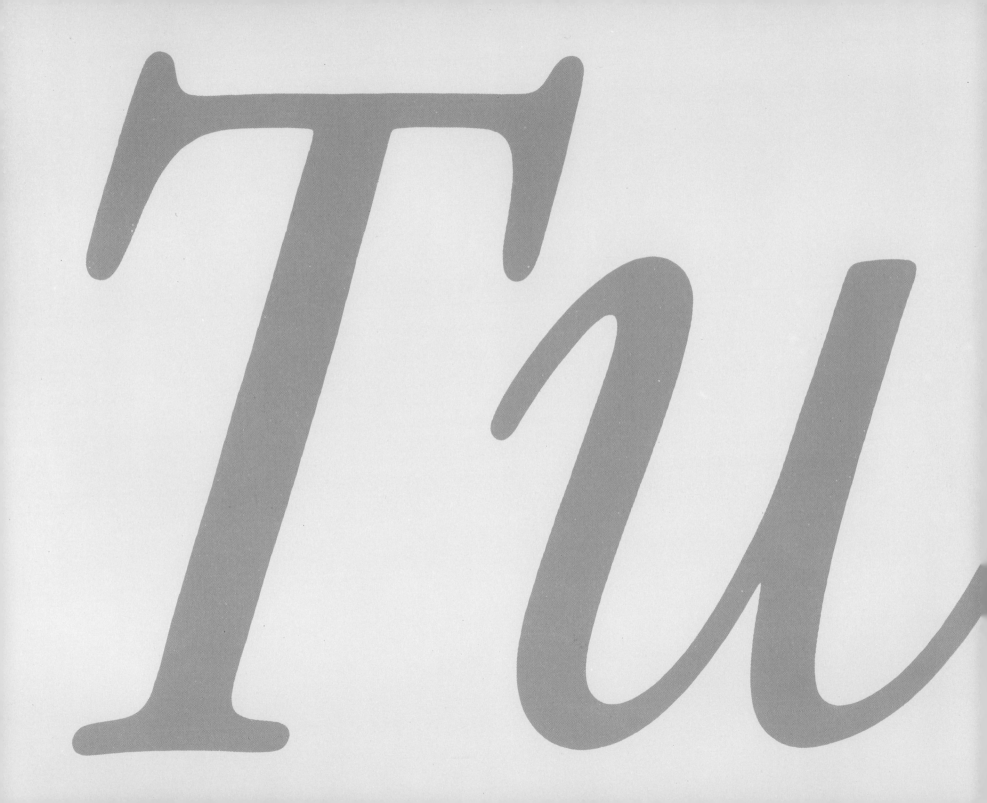

The Basics of Ornamental Grass Gardening

Garden Design by Oehme, van Sweden & Associates, Inc.

*I*t is as difficult to imagine the garden devoid of grasses as it is to imagine man's history without wheat, corn, paper, sugarcane, bamboo, and reeds. In the garden, the primary function of grass is as a lawn. But even in the maintenance of the garden we use bamboo rakes and stakes, lay salt hay on as mulch, and protect our heads with straw hats. In plantings, grasses can serve as screens—ascending over fifteen feet (4.5 metres) in the air—to block out the neighbours' houses or a busy street. It has been said that certain species of bamboo can rise to over a hundred feet (30 metres) in their native environment. But of all these garden uses, perhaps the most amazing is that grasses can function as ornamentals, taking their place in the flower bed with a beauty that matches the most exquisite flowers. Grasses were first introduced as greens or lawns ("lawn" is derived from the Celtic "lann" [a derivative of land], meaning "enclosure"). These closely mown grass expanses were grown for ornamental or recreational use.

The idea of using lawn grasses came about for both practical and

*L*ong relegated to the lawn, grasses are being used more and more to create interesting textures and accents in the garden. Above: Ornamental grasses are successfully used to contrast a green lawn and a mass of black-eyed Susans. Opposite page: *Phalaris arundinacea* 'Picta' (Ribbon Grass) is one of the most popular ornamental grasses, although it should be planted with plenty of space around it or in underground containers to help curb its invasive nature.

Garden Design by Thomas A. Reinhardt

aesthetic reasons. People needed a simple, practical surface surrounding the house for recreation and space. The beauty of a cut or grazed meadow provided a ready solution. Grass felt good underfoot, retained its beauty despite frequent mowings, and required little besides watering and mowing. In many countries, lawns were first introduced in public parks.

Lawn grasses grow from basal meristems that are not lost to mechanical mowing; however, not all grasses can survive repeated mowings and therefore can't serve as lawns. Lawn grasses, like other grasses, are valuable to the environment. They control erosion, hold down dust, and help regulate soil- and air-moisture levels.

Grasses function not only as lawns but also as ground covers. Unlike lawn grasses, ground-cover grasses are allowed to grow to their natural form. These are grass genera and species that best retain their natural form for aesthetic and botanical reasons. Ribbon Grass, or Gardener's Garters (*Phalaris arundinacea* 'Picta'), with its lovely variegated foliage and ivory-white broad blades, forms thick one-to-two-foot-high (30-to-60-centimetre) ground-cover expanses. As is the case with *Phalaris*, many ground-cover grasses make lovely carpets. If successful, they grow so thick that one cannot see the soil beneath. Ground-cover grasses grow either from running rhizomes (a horizontal stem on or under the ground that sends up a succession of leaves or stems at the apex) or from clumps.

Tufted species, such as Blue Fescue (*Festuca glauca*), send out leaves or stems from one central core. The foliage from these species grows from the clump and hangs over the ground, covering it and becoming part of a single mass when planted along with others.

Running-rhizome varieties, on the other hand, form a thick carpet from underground or overground rhizomes, generating a network of attached plants that grow from and into one another. In both rhizome and tufted varieties, the ground-cover grasses serve to retard and prevent weed growth.

The reasons why ground-cover grasses cannot serve as lawn grasses are not simply aesthetic ones. Ground-cover grasses, with their high meristems (undifferentiated tissue that is capable of developing into various other tissues or plant organs), cannot be frequently or closely cut. Such cuttings damage the meristems, prevent growth, and eventually kill the plant. Meristems on lawn grasses, on the other hand, are very low, located just above the ground. In this case, frequent cuttings invigorate the growth of the grass.

Blue Fescue works well as a ground cover. Its densely clustered blades form a neat, almost circular mound. Its delicate and slender leaf blades contrast well against broad-leafed perennials. Blue fescue keeps its marked blue colour throughout the year. It looks attractive against green and yellow foliage, and alongside flowering perennials and dwarf 'shrubs. At only six to eight inches (15 to 20 centimetres), it makes a nice edging. In terms of design it is advisable to use all ground covers in combination with taller, more vertical elements. Various combinations of ground-cover grasses can

*B*lue Fescue, shown here in its flowering state, is an excellent ground cover that contrasts nicely with broad-leafed perennials.

28

IMPORTANT ORNAMENTAL GRASSES

CHINESE SILVER GRASS
Miscanthus sinensis

Grown for its stately size, its dense and generally U-shaped form with arching blades.

BLUE FESCUE
Festuca glauca

Known for its appealing blue foliage and low, dense mounds.

PAMPAS GRASS
Cortaderia selloana

The queen of the ornamental grasses, with tall and erect silver-white to pink plumes.

SEDGE
Carex

The forest grasses noted for their foliage. Likes moist soil.

FOUNTAIN GRASS
Pennisetum alopecuroides

Characterized by globed mounds with straight culms and dense spikelike bottle-brush inflorescences (flowers).

BAMBOO
Bambuseae

Mostly woody grasses. Tall, erect, with multiple leaf blades, which are borne at nodes that are located at periodic distances along the stem. Most originate in the Orient, where they are highly valued.

RIBBON GRASS
Phalaris arundinaceae 'Picta'

Spreading from rhizomes, which are ground covers, the most valued being the ivory variegated type. Medium high, with broad blades.

SWITCH GRASS
Panicum

Mostly cylindrical, erect form, with loosely formed inflorescences. Known for its bright red autumn colour.

*Throughout the book both common and botanical names are included where appropriate.
For cross-reference, check the index or Chapter IV, "A Catalogue of Ornamental Grasses."

Members of the *Miscanthus* species, right, are favourites of designers because of their stately presence and silky panicles. Far right: The soft, airy appearance of *Panicum virgatum* (left) is a nice contrast to the erect lines of the *Calamagrostis acutiflora* 'Stricta' (right). The contrast of textures and shapes is one of the most appealing aspects of gardening with ornamental grasses.

be used to create a patterned effect.

In addition to ground covers, ornamental grasses work well as specimens. Some of the nicest are of the *Miscanthus* genus. Their slender flower stems, silky panicles, and long blades make them a favourite of the designer. *Miscanthus* works especially well as an accent plant, dramatizing the perennial border or bed. It also fits well into a sitting area where the sound of the wind through the blades can be heard. Light sparkles on the blades, glistening with each movement of the wind. *Miscanthus* goes well with boulders and water, and is striking against gravel, driftwood, or a background of mass plantings. Its height and delicate, long blades evoke the feeling of the prairie. In the winter, when all else is gone but the silhouette of leafless trees, its brown panicles flowing in the wind make a beautiful accent and give the quiet feeling of Monet's haystacks. Moreover, it is a grass that, when set against the background of ground covers, appears like a fountain spraying ripples of softly flowing water.

Ornamental grasses evoke the wild feeling of nature—its freedom, vitality, stillness, and movement—as well as the more formal, controlled feeling of the garden. The vastness of the wheat field is reflected in the solitary high ornamental, while the waves in the sea are reflected in the effect of the wind in the high grass.

Unlike perennials, which bloom and then disappear, making way for the next stage in the garden, ornamental grasses are a fixed element, enduring the entire growing season and continuing into winter. They are a timeless element, because flowering is not the only reason for their inclusion, and because they endure with little change throughout the season. Another great aspect of grasses is that they combine delicacy with fullness. They are stable, enduring, and alive—their beauty and appearance react to the wind and the light. While perennials and annuals can lose the flavour of their natural habitat, grasses, even under the calculated control of a designer, retain their wild character. Beach grasses call forth the memory of the ocean. Bamboo holds the image of the East, especially of Japan. Switch Grass (*Panicum virgatum*) evokes the prairie, Dwarf Papyrus the Nile delta. Bog grasses planted in wet, springlike areas in the garden bring on the feeling of the wet moorland and hollows, while woodrushes call forth the deep shade of a woodland canopy.

The designer who works with ornamental grasses and grasslike plants should investigate the natural habitat of the plant, and incorporate the information into the design concept.

Garden Design by Oehme, van Sweden & Associates, Inc.

ORNAMENTAL GRASSES IN THE GARDEN

Until now, ornamental grasses have been used somewhat sparingly by landscape architects and designers, yet there are many advantages to including them in a landscape design.

First of all, they are relatively easy to maintain. Because of their role as pioneer in natural habitats, grasses have developed into very hardy, self-sufficient plants.

Secondly, grasses are attractive in all four seasons. Unlike many plants, they are not at their peak in the spring, but are at full growth during the summer months. Some varieties change colour, and flower late, remaining beautiful even when their foliage turns brown. In the winter, when other perennials are absent, the golden foliage of died-back ornamental grass creates a stunning presence in a stark landscape.

Thirdly, ornamental grasses bring a natural element into the garden. The wild and free nature of ornamental grasses combined with the more formal elements of the landscape such as perennials and lawn grasses, or structures such as pools and patios creates a pleasant juxtaposition between the spontaneity of nature and the control of a landscaped garden.

Lastly, ornamental grasses are among the most versatile plants used in landscaping. There are ornamental grasses for almost any environment. Some species grow naturally in the dunes and can be planted directly into sharply draining sand or soil. Others are suitable for bog conditions and will thrive in and around landscape pools and water gardens.

ORNAMENTAL GRASSES AS GROUND COVERS

Ground-cover plantings should be interesting yet not overly dominant in a landscape plan. Dynamic yet subtle, ground covers are devices that pull together a multitude of garden elements. They can create space, and, when used imaginatively in combination with other types of plants, they can create a picture of harmonizing shapes, textures, and colours.

It is important to point out that with ground covers, as with any planting, the designer should find out the optimum conditions under which these plants grow. Few things are as disturbing as poorly grown plants. Especially disheartening is a ground cover that never really covers anything.

The most valuable ground-cover grasslike plants are members of the genuses *Carex*, *Luzula*, and *Festuca*. Many species of *Carex* and *Luzula* thrive in the partial shade of woodland settings, where the

Garden Design by Oehme, van Sweden & Associates, Inc.

*B*ecause of their self-sufficiency, longevity, adaptability, and versatility, ornamental grasses are being used more and more in the landscape or garden—whether they are used as specimens in the perennial garden (opposite page) or as a ground cover along a walk (above).

soil is rich in organic matter. The species of *Festuca* prefer full sun in a sandy soil with humus mixed in. (See page 118 for a list of good ground-cover grasses.)

ORNAMENTAL GRASSES AS SPECIMENS

Certain grasses can be used to accentuate specific areas in the garden and to help build up or contribute to a desired atmosphere. For example, tall specimens of ornamental grasses work well when used in, or around, sitting areas, patios, ponds, and recreational areas; as accents within the garden; or as focal points in a well-designed landscape.

Because of their extraordinary appearance (size, shape, texture, and colour), many ornamental grasses are used as specimen plants in plantings of perennials or woody ornamentals. The tall-growing species of the grass family work well as screens, either in the form of a hedgerow or in a more natural, grouped planting. Here is something that can replace the privet hedge! (See page 118 for a list of specimen plantings.)

ORNAMENTAL GRASSES FOR ROCK GARDENS

Ornamental grasses work well when used to contrast the cushion-like effect of rock garden plantings. Attractive throughout most of the growing season, they help keep the rock garden interesting in late summer when most of the rock garden plants are past their prime. Ornamental grasses serve as intermediaries between the small- and medium-sized perennials.

When incorporating grasses in a rock garden, do not plant them close to the more delicate and slow-growing perennials. Many ornamental grasses will create heavy root competition that will suppress the growth of tender perennials. (See page 118 for a list of rock garden grasses.)

ORNAMENTAL GRASSES IN THE NATURAL OR WILD GARDEN

The use of native grasses evokes the feeling of the countryside. As natural gardens are becoming increasingly popular, more and more landscape designers are incorporating such grasses for their natural effect. The two most important factors to a successful natural garden are full, direct sunlight and well-drained, sandy soil enriched with humus.

*A*chnatherum calamagrostis (Silver Spike Grass), opposite page left, makes an excellent specimen with its sweeping panicles and long decorative season. Opposite page right: In addition to specimen plantings, ornamental grasses are widely used in borders and along walkways. Left: With its long arching panicles in their full glory, *Pennisetum setaceum* (Crimson Fountain Grass) adds a stately elegance to the garden. Below: When combined with other plantings, ornamental grasses are an integral part of the perennial border.

Garden Design by Meadowbrook Farm, Pennsylvania

Garden Design by Oehme, van Sweden & Associates, Inc.

Garden Design by Oehme, van Sweden & Associates, Inc.

*B*ecause of their resilience and adaptability, ornamental grasses, sedges, and rushes will survive where other perennials may perish. Above: In the woodland garden, grasses can cope with shade and moderate root competition. While in the seaside garden (opposite page) they can withstand the harsh conditions of salt air, droughts, and major temperature shifts.

Spring to early summer is the peak period for such a garden, when the wild tulips, onion Iris, flowering Allium, and pulsatilla are in their prime. During this time, grasses such as Sheep's Fescue (*Festuca ovina*) help to highlight and enhance the rural feeling of the garden. And, as in other types of garden styles, ornamental grasses help carry natural gardens through the nonpeak seasons as well. (See page 118 for a list of grasses for the natural or wild garden.)

ORNAMENTAL GRASSES FOR THE WOODLAND GARDEN

In the woodland garden ornamental grasses and sedges enhance the natural character of a landscape design. Here, mostly members of the sedge family are used. In general, sedges can cope with shade and the moderate root competition of woodland trees. Sedges, whether planted in smaller groups or en masse as a ground cover, combine well with other typical woodland perennials. The foliage of sedges placed next to a foliage of ferns brings about interesting effects and contrasts. The variegated cultivars of sedges in particular, with their light foliage colours, create highlights in the dim, shady woodland. The soil for woodland plantings should be prepared with a considerable amount of organic matter—preferably with leaf mould. *Deschampsia caespitosa* (Gramineae family) is an extremely valuable plant for the partially shaded woodland. (See page 118 for a list of ornamental grasses for the woodland garden.)

ORNAMENTAL GRASSES FOR THE COASTAL GARDEN

Coastal plants must be able to withstand extremely harsh conditions—salt air, droughts, major shifts in temperature, fierce winds, and ocean storms. Very few plants can survive, let alone thrive, in such conditions, and even the survivors can succumb to occasional hurricanes and severe storms. In such an environment plant selection depends more on survivability than on aesthetics.

Coastal plants that do survive these conditions are essential to soil stabilization. Homes located close to the coast cannot afford to risk erosion. In such a context, it is difficult to overestimate the importance of European Beach Grass (*Elymus arenarius*). Found along sandy beaches it is nature's stabilizer and seashore pioneer, as well as a possessor of austere beauty.

Other grasses, such as *Festuca*,

Garden Design by Thomas A. Feinhardt

Phalaris, *Panicum*, and *Elymus*, also work well as dune plantings; however, they prefer richer soils and are 'pocket planted' for best results. To do this, dig a planting hole twice the size of the root ball of the grass and replace the sand with a mixture of one part soil and one part organic material. This provides a good soil base for the plants. (See page 119 for a list of coastal grasses.)

GRASSES FOR THE EDGE OF PONDS, SHALLOW WATER, AND BOGS

If your garden has a pond, grasses are wonderful plantings for the edge or in shallow water areas. They help to naturalize and harmonize the effect of ponds and aquatic plantings. *Arundo donax*, *Sinarundinaria nitida*, *Spartina pectinata* and cultivars, as well as many species and cultivars of *Miscanthus* can be planted in the environmental conditions prevailing at the water edges of ponds and streams. Many members of the sedge and the rush families can be planted into boggy conditions and even into shallow water. If the area of the waterside garden is extensive, then quickly spreading *Phragmites australis* is appropriate. *P. australis* can not only grow in bogs, but in standing water as well. Associated readily with natural habitats, its use will introduce a wild feeling to the garden.

GRASSES FOR THE PERENNIAL BORDER

Flowering as well as foliage perennials can be successfully combined with ornamental grasses. The full, rippling heads of ornamental grasses appear like spraying fountains when interspersed with foliage plants. The bold, shapely leaves of foliage perennials provide a pleasing contrast with the narrow leaves and pale, pendulous stems of ornamental grasses. A few examples of foliage perennials that can be used for this type of planting are: *Hosta* species and cultivars, *Ligularia* species and cultivars, and *Rodgersia* species. (See page 119 for a list of grasses for the perennial border.)

Garden Design by Thomas A. Reinhardt

*P*halaris arundinacea (Ribbon Grass), left, is a versatile grass that is as effective by the waterside as it is in the perennial border. Right: One of the greatest attributes of ornamental grasses is that they successfully combine with flowering as well as foliage perennials.

Garden Design by Thomas A. Reinhard*

39

*A*lthough they require very little maintenance, some grasses are rhizomatous and can be very invasive. Above: *Phalaris arundinacea* (Ribbon Grass) should be planted in bottomless containers to keep growth under control. Left: *Imperata cylindrica* 'Red Baron' (Japanese Blood Grass) is a rhizomatous grass that is slow growing and not very invasive.

Working with Ornamental Grasses

In general, ornamental grasses are low-maintenance plants. They usually do not require any deadheading or staking and they are almost never attacked by pests or diseases. But the gardener does need to know how to plant them, how and when to divide them, when to cut them back, and what fertilizer they require.

Tall ornamental grasses are usually planted 4 to 5 feet (1.2 to 1.5 metres) apart; smaller species are planted closer—from 1 to 2 ½ feet (30 to 76 centimetres) apart, depending on the species. If the grasses are planted too closely, the effect of the individual plants is lost and the plants are weakened, because of too much root competition. The best time for planting grasses is in spring or early summer. Though there are species that can be planted bare root, it is best to plant container-grown grasses. The following species should *never* be planted bare root:

Arrhenatherum elatius bulbosum
  'Variegatum'
Carex (most species and cultivars)
Festuca species and cultivars
Luzula nivea
Luzula sylvatica and cultivars
Sesleria species
Arundinaria pygmaea
Sinarundinaria species
Stipa species

Most ornamental grasses require pocket planting with fifty per cent topsoil (which should be on the sandy side) and fifty per cent organic material. Many ornamental grasses are heavy feeders, and after they have used up all the nutrition in the ground where they were planted, they start to grow outward, leaving the centre section bare. When this happens, it is time to dig out the clump of grass, divide it, and discard the core. Then pocket replant a part of the division. Though ornamental grasses require fertile soil, the gardener has to be careful not to give them too much nitrogen. Over-fertilization with nitrogen forces them to grow too rapidly, making them weak and unhealthy.

Though most ornamental grasses are so tough that they knock out weed growth, it is advisable to mulch in order to improve the soil structure and to supply nutrients in a natural form. Mulch also stabilizes soil moisture and temperature, and suppresses weed

growth in spring and early summer, when the grasses are not yet fully grown.

Ornamental grasses are some of the very few perennials that are four-season plants. After grasses are cut back in the spring, it takes only a couple of weeks for new leaves to emerge. By the middle of summer the grasses reach their full size. They provide beauty from then through the autumn and even in their dormant stage during winter. Large, established clumps of grasses can be cut back with electric hedge trimmers.

To contain plantings of invasive running bamboos (e.g. *Phyllostachys*) or running ornamental grasses (e.g. *Phalaris*), plant them using a barrier: a fibreglass panel, large pots or buckets with the bottoms cut out, or pieces of large plastic drainpipe. Unwanted shoots of running bamboo can be controlled by cutting them with a

*D*eschampsia caespitosa (Tufted Hair Grass), which can be propagated by either division or seed, is a good grass for a partially shaded woodland. Right: *Phyllostachys,* a running bamboo, should be planted behind an underground barrier or in a bottomless pot to curb its invasiveness. Far right: Members of the *Carex* species can be propagated by either division or seed.

lawn mower on a regular basis.

Most ornamental grasses should be propagated by division. The best time to do this is in the spring, when the soil has warmed up and the new growth has appeared. To ensure a successful propagation, the divisions should not be too small, and the roots of the divisions should not be root pruned. Dividing is done with a very sharp spade or, in the case of established plants with hard root balls, an axe. The divisions should be planted in the ground or potted immediately and well watered. Be sure to keep them moist until they are well established.

The following grasses can be propagated from seed:

Andropogon scoparius
Bouteloua species
Briza maxima
Briza media
Carex species
Deschampsia caespitosa
Eragrostis trichodes
Festuca mairei
Helictotrichon sempervirens
Hordeum jubalum
Hystrix patula
Juncus effusus
Luzula species
Molinia species
Pennisetum orientale
Pennisetum setaceum
Poa chaixii
Stipa species
Uniola latifolia

Thr

ee Designing with Ornamental Grasses

*T*he adaptability and variety of ornamental grasses presents the designer with a wide range of landscape possibilities. Not only can grasses add new and varied elements to the formal landscape, they also can add an entirely new dimension of naturalized designs. Grasses can be used alone, in groupings, in combination with other grasses, or as complements to many types of perennials or shrubs. The hardiness of grasses allows the designer to increase the range of conditions and locations for plantings. Moreover, their low-maintenance advantages can be utilized by the landscape architect responsible for public or commercial projects.

This chapter serves as an introduction to the world of ornamental grass design. We can only give the reader a feeling for the number of possible applications and for the interesting effects that can be achieved.

FIGURE 3-1

Garden Design by Oehme, van Sweden & Associates, Inc.

FIGURE 3-2

Simple Designs

Many ornamental grasses combine well with annuals. For example, Fountain Grass (*Pennisetum setaceum*) (Figure 3-1) brings a soft delicate backdrop to the bright red colour of zinnias planted en masse. The contrasts in height, colour, movement, texture, and shape make this combination especially exciting. Such contrasts create a harmony of composition. For example, the movement of the grass contrasts and complements the more stable, erect line of the zinnias. In addition, there is a strong contrast between the naturalness of the grass and the more formal, cultivated feel of the zinnias. The effective use of contrasts such as these is one of the most important aspects of ornamental grass gardening. These contrasts are illustrated in many of the other pictures in this section.

One final note about this composition: The red cannas that lighten the background of rich green trees add balance to the design by framing the grass and providing foliage contrast.

Ornamental grasses can be used to break up ground-cover plantings and provide a focal centre for a composition. In Figure 3-2, the ground cover *Sedum* gives a nice carpet effect, which is broken by the round clump of the low-growing *Festuca glauca*. This low-growing mix brings about a merging of the contrasting foliage through a natural, serene flow. The blue shade of the *Festuca* blends well with the purple bloom of the *Sedum*, while the foliage of the *Sedum* provides an appropriate backdrop for the thin, pendular blades of the *Festuca*.

Striped Eulalia Grass (*Miscanthus sinensis* 'Variegatus') has a graceful appearance. Its pendular, fountainlike shape, combined with its good height, makes it a dominant element in a landscape design. Often used in groupings, the Eulalia has a distinctively natural look, calling forth the prairie or the bank of a pond. It also combines well with a wide variety of ground covers, its height emphasized by the low-growing carpet. But Eulalia can also be placed in a perennial planting, where erect elements and colour play an important part. In Figure 3-3, Eulalia is combined with the radiant yellow of flowering black-eyed Susan (*Rudbeckia*). Both of these plants grow well in partial shade and, because of their bright appearance, are able to light up darker areas in front of tall trees or other verdant settings. Each enhances the unique

FIGURE 3-3

character of the other rather than merging and harmonizing, thus achieving a structurally interesting accent or focus.

Grasses can be effectively integrated into a wide variety of perennial and annual plantings. They make interesting ground covers and can create a low-growing background for other, taller flowering plants. One of the most effective ornamental grass ground covers is Ribbon Grass (*Phalaris arundinaria* 'Picta'). It is a rampant grower and often must be controlled through thinning and dividing. Growing to a height of about one foot (31 centimetres), it quickly spreads to cover bare areas. Its light, variegated, sometimes ivory-coloured blades are a splendid backdrop for darker foliage or bright flowers. In Figure 3-4, Ribbon Grass is used as part of a foundation planting. It is combined with *Heliopsis,* cosmos, snapdragons, and black-eyed Susans to bring about a closely knit bed. Planting Ribbon Grass among such perennials in a casual structure creates the ambience of a cottage garden.

As we have seen, ornamental grasses create interesting effects when combined with ground covers, annuals, and perennials. They can also be combined with other grasses, shrubs, and trees, producing many interesting contrasts in texture, colour, and shape. For example, ornamental grasses, when

FIGURE 3-4

FIGURE 3-5

planted with evergreen trees, provide a textural foil to the rigid vertical lines of the evergreen.

A stark contrast between grasses and evergreens is evident in Figure 3-5. Here, an established clump of Chinese Silver Grass (*Miscanthus sinensis*) is yellowish in comparison with the rich greens and bluish hues of the evergreens. Balance is achieved by positioning the evergreens so that they frame the grass. The Chinese Silver Grass (*Miscanthus sinensis*) then becomes a compositional axis, with its colour differentiation highlighting the dark background.

The larger ornamental grasses, such as *Miscanthus sinensis* or *Miscanthus floridulus*, can be combined with evergreens to form natural screens. The grasses serve to fill in the lower areas of the screen and to add varieties of texture and shape. Unlike the sharp contrasts of the former illustration, the ornamental grasses in Figure 3-6 are blended into the landscape. The grasses form a low bordering screen, while the taller evergreens provide a more effective screen in the background. Here, the ornamental grasses are planted in a group; *Miscanthus floridulus* and others combine to form a pleasing border. They complement the tall evergreen screen by providing a gradually evolving vertical movement that is less harsh and intimidating. By merging into the back-

ground green, the grasses evoke a quiet mood while still retaining their characteristic difference in texture and shape. This blending is enhanced through the use of ornamental grasses of varying heights as a border to small shrubs and a grass lawn.

The wide variety of available ornamental grasses presents the designer with a myriad of options in creating beautiful and original garden designs. The previous photographs in this chapter have shown examples of ornamental grasses combined with other types of plants. The next few examples will look at the use of different types of ornamental grasses combined with each other.

Grasses may not add radiant colour the way annual or perennial common flowers do, but their contributions in terms of texture, shape, movement, and even sound are reason enough to create landscapes that are solely or largely made up of grasses. A simple demonstration of the beauty and gracefulness that the combination of two or three grasses can create is found in Figure 3-7. Here, a lovely annual grass is planted along with Swamp Foxtail Grass (*Pennisetum alopecuroides*). The creamy white spikes make a pleasing colour contrast with the purple-brown spikes of the Fountain Grass. Their similar texture and shape brings about a oneness and continuity. When the

wind moves across the planting it responds like a field of wheat or rye swaying to and fro, like the waves of the sea. Here, the gardener uses a mass of grasses to mimic the prairie and the loveliness of the grain fields.

Grasses with entirely different textures and forms can combine to create interesting and dynamic

compositions. The combination of Ribbon Grass (*Phalaris arundinacea* 'Picta') with Tufted Hair Grass (*Deschampsia caepitosa*) and Porcupine Grass (*Miscanthus sinensis* 'Strictus') uses sharp contrasts without causing disharmony. The fuzzy cloudlike appearance of the mass planting of Swamp Foxtail Grass adds delicacy and airiness to

FIGURE 3-6

FIGURE 3-8

FIGURE 3-7

the heavy, rugged lines of the ivory Ribbon Grass. The erect lines of the Porcupine Grass in the far background add textures and colours, while balancing the contrasting weight of the other two grasses.

A wild, almost untouched path cuts through the heart of the grass garden in Figure 3-9. The effect was achieved through careful planning and by placing ornamental grasses at strategic points. This is a perfect example of a carefully

FIGURE 3-9

planned landscape that evokes a wild, natural look. The selection and positioning of the grass specimens were done in a manner that appears to be random; however, the organic, natural feeling is attained quite intentionally. Here the designer used grasses that do not have a well-defined form and do not act as focal points but rather blend into the natural surrounding.

A lovely organic composition formed from several ornamental grasses (Ribbon Grass, Swamp Fox-tail Grass, and *Miscanthus*) is illustrated in Figure 3-10. The purple, blue, creamy white, and green colours of the grasses intermix and merge to create a soft, dreamlike atmosphere. Although placed in groups, none of the grasses stand out or distract attention from the whole. Rather, each grouping correlates to the next, and fits into the totality of the arrangement. Also note that the design was conceived in three tiers, each building up to the next, giving perspective, depth, and space. Too often, design errors lead to specimens being obscured—smaller plants positioned behind larger ones, one type of plant crowding another. Here, however, ample space is given to each group, and the middle level harmonizes the other two by using similar elements that soften the strong contrasts between the front and rear planting.

Simple designs in the immediate vicinity of the home can have tremendous impact when located in the midst of the lawn. Often the space used for lawn area in the front or rear of the house is too important to be left solely to the simple, monotonous character of lawns. Even where the lawn area has been structured by irregular edgings, the garden may still be passive, plain, and lacking in visual impact. Planting beds in the midst

FIGURE 3-10

Garden Design by Thomas A. Reinhardt

FIGURE 3-11

of the lawn area will help break the monotony of a lawn. This planting should be dynamic yet not overwhelming; it should have significant form yet not be so high as to become a visual obstruction. Trees or shrubs are often used to build vertical elements in the vast horizontal surface of lawns, but in the immediate vicinity of the home, where space may be limited, such dominant plantings can be out of place. Small beds are cosier and more intimate. They do not cut the space or the view from the house, and they are not out of proportion with the dimensions of the house or property. In such instances the use of grasses is essential. Ornamental grasses provide planting beds with interesting colour and significant texture and body while contributing to the aesthetic character of the bed.

In Figure 3-11, a grouping of *Festuca glauca* is used in an island planting, combined with low sedums and dwarf carnations. The bluish foliage of the *Festuca* and the carnations complement each other, whereas the finely textured Blue Fescue contrasts with the textures of the carnations and sedums, and with the lawn. Bluish-green foliage is always a welcome contribution to any landscape design where the range of foliage colour is limited. *Festuca glauca* is a good choice for creating interesting colour and texture contrasts.

Ornamental Grasses and Fixed Structural Elements

One of the major problems facing garden designers is the way in which fixed structures such as paths, driveways, patios, porches, fences, gates, walls, garages, and houses interact with the land-scaped environment. Most of the time, the landscaping will take a backseat to these fixed structural elements. Houses, paths, and paved driveways will probably be in place prior to the general landscaping. This unfortunate situation confronts the designer with rigid, fixed, immovable elements that must be incorporated in the design. In these cases, the selection of plants will aim at screening, concealing, or softening these given fixtures in an attempt to integrate them with the landscape. Sometimes one of the main purposes of landscaping the property will be to humanize or soften these fixtures and to make the immediate vicinity of the home environment more livable. In fortunate circumstances, the planning of the house and garden will be integrated from the beginning. The designer will be working prior to the installation of the fixed structures, and sometimes can work out his design in conjunction with the design of the house itself. In these cases, the designer will be faced with fewer difficulties but still must use all the skills he or she might possess to bring man-made materials into harmony with nature.

Instead of hiding the fixed architectural elements, the garden designer might instead want to emphasize some of them, while de-emphasizing others—gates, for example, may take on a dominant position, whereas driveways may be screened and hidden. The designer must also give considerable thought to the way in which these two worlds can be integrated. Geometric shapes have to harmonize with the undulating lines of nature, and man-made materials or painted surfaces must be incorporated into the colours and textures of nature. While there are cases where the designer chooses to highlight the contrasts, often an attempt is made to use the natural to soften or cancel the man-made. In all cases, careful thought must be given to the effect and to the appropriate combination of plants that will best serve these ends.

Ornamental grasses, by providing greater choices and a wider

*F*inding a way to naturalize or camouflage the intrusion of fixed structural elements in a garden or landscape can pose major problems. Ornamental grasses are effective tools for softening the hard edges of a walkway.

Garden Design by Oehme, van Sweden & Associates, Irc.

*T*his design, left, successfully combines ornamental grasses, foliage and flowering perennials, a slate walk, and a simple arbor to create a pleasant garden walk.

range of conditions, allow the designer more versatility. But they do more than just add new choices: Grasses achieve aesthetic effects that might be essential for solving the specific problems that the designer faces. The majority of grasses add movement and airiness to the landscape. They soften harsh, rigid contours and add a natural feeling to architectural forms. Less massive than many shrubs and evergreen trees, grasses are also less static. They can be used to partially conceal structures, allowing fixtures to be visible without being dominant. Decorative and graceful, they add beauty without attracting too much attention, a consideration when the fixture they are hiding is not to become overtly apparent or conspicuous. Moreover, grasses are ideally suited to create a country-or cottage like feeling. They add warmth and intimacy to the home environment by evoking the peaceful and quiet world of nature.

The natural, cottagelike effect is evident in the following set of photographs. A stepping-stone path and country-style house (Figure 3-12) are partially screened by Swamp Foxtail Grass (*Pennisetum alopecuroides*). The well-established *Pennisetum* has actually overgrown the path, presenting the walker with a bit of a problem, especially after rain or irrigation. Yet the aesthetic charm of these grasses is appropriate for paths and driveways. Planted in mass they soften the rigid lines of the blue stone driveway in Figure 3-13. Their drooping blades present a wild yet warm and intimate feeling. Dynamic and abundant, they help correct the problems of an overly

FIGURE 3-12

Garden Design by Oehme, van Sweden & Associates, Inc.

FIGURE 3-13

FIGURE 3-14

FIGURE 3-15

visible driveway. In a third setting (Figure 3-14), the *Pennisetum* softens the trellis walls and brick columns by virtue of its arching habit and delicate foliage texture. The strong contrast in terms of foliage colour and foliage texture between *Pennisetum* and the Red Barberry in the corner makes for an interesting composition, though the narrowness of the bed is a difficult space to work with. The Red Barberry echoes the red of the brick walk and columns while the *Pennisetum* complements the green of the vine behind it. Notice, too, how the *Pennisetum* and the Red Barberry soften and integrate the brick path, transforming straight lines into soft, graceful, undulating curves.

Ornamental grasses also work well in front of walls, helping to soften them and integrate them into the surrounding area. Even in a narrow bed, Ribbon Grass (*Phalaris arundinacea* 'Picta') can light up the entire planting, tying the white of the fence, door, and window to the white in the planting (see Figure 3-15). The grass's variegated foliage goes well with the dark-brown wooden shingles of the house. Its arching blades, with their height and downward tension, tie together the house and the path. Ribbon Grass has a texture and movement that brings vitality into this otherwise overly calculated design.

In a less dramatic fashion, *Molinia* is used as a specimen in front of a house (Figure 3-16). Its delicate, airy foliage softens the heavy corner of the house while its texture corresponds nicely to the daylilies planted along the steps. It is a lovely sight to sit on the porch and look out through the loose panicle, watching the gentle movement of the grass in the wind as the filtered light sets the grass aglow.

Even in the midst of winter, a single grass can have an immense effect upon an urbanized landscape. In Figure 3-17, the warm, golden panicle of Maiden Grass (*Miscanthus sinensis* 'Gracillimus') is shown before the dark, rigid brick wall of a house. The golden hues are harmonious with the red brick and the white snow. The stately power of the dormant grass reflects the peace of winter and

FIGURE 3-16

FIGURE 3-17

offers an intimation of the coming springtime.

Striped Eulalia Grass (*Miscanthus sinensis* 'Variegatus') is a lovely plant to use as a specimen. Its white-green variegation presents dynamic foliage, and its arching yet clearly vertical disposition balances horizontal and vertical elements of a composition, making it ideal to plant in front of low fences. In Figure 3-18, the grass has a pronounced sculptural effect, acting as the focal point of a perennial mixed planting. The touch of white in the foliage echoes the delicate design of the white fence.

Whereas the Striped Eulalia Grass in Figure 3-18 is used as a specimen to accent a white fence, the Chinese Silver Grass (*Miscanthus sinensis*) in Figure 3-19 is planted en masse and is used to partially obscure the cold metallic effect of the black fence and driveway. Though the planting bed is rather narrow, the ornamental grasses radically alter the regimented and depressing feel of metal bars and asphalt. The foliage enlivens and naturalizes this picture, with the blade tips descending onto the driveway surface.

Ornamental grasses have a particularly nice effect when planted along paths and walks. Using flowers to border a walk often looks too cultivated; the bright colours of the flowers contrast too sharply with the man-made walk.

FIGURE 3-18

FIGURE 3-19

Grasses, on the other hand, tend to merge with the path or walk. Instead of emphasizing the contrast in materials, grasses soften the division. An interesting effect is achieved by mixing grasses with annual flowering plants such as asters. In Figure 3-20, Ribbon Grass envelops the flowers, creating the effect of a flower bouquet. The grass also softens the contrast between the flowers and the cobblestone walk—its variegated blades highlighting a dark corner.

Whereas the use of dense ground covers such as ivy or sedum tends to delineate the shape of paths and walks, ornamental grasses usually work to obscure the line. This is illustrated by the contrasting effect of Tufted Hair Grass (*Deschampsia caespitosa*) and ivy on the slate walk in Figure 3-21. The combination of grass and ivy provides a pleasing contrast with daylilies and Lily turf, emphasizing the variation in foliage. However, this usual aesthetic contrast between grasses and denser ground covers does not always hold true. Grasses such as Pygmy Bamboo (*Arundinaria pygmaea*) can be used to create a dense carpet (see Figure 3-22). A mass planting of Pygmy Bamboo is similar to ivy in that it acts as a weed barrier and has a calm, soothing appeal.

The clean lines that play an important role in the last two designs are abandoned for a wilder,

FIGURE 3-20

FIGURE 3-21

more natural path in the next two photographs. In Figure 3-23, a slate path is bordered by an astilbe planting on one side and a variety of ornamental grasses on the other. Maiden Grass is used as a specimen, its foliage looming higher than the surrounding grasses. Behind this specimen is the yellow background of black-eyed Susans adding color to this fine play of texture and foliage effects. Figure 3-24 is a masterful example of grasses used to give graceful outlines of a natural stylized path mulched with wood chips. Fountain Grass and Ribbon Grass are used successfully as underplantings for the shrubs. Here, the designer creates visual interest through foliage contrasts alone, with only a touch of colour highlighting the many green hues. The designer accomplishes a wild, uncalculated

FIGURE 3-22

FIGURE 3-23

design by setting plants so that they grow out onto the path. Yet the undulations have a distinct rhythm, with the final bend breaking the visual continuity and suggesting a hidden dense woodland path lying just beyond.

As we can see from these illustrations, ornamental grasses can be used to border a variety of paths and walks, from the formal to the fully natural. These effects can also

Garden Design by Thomas A. Reinhardt

FIGURE 3-24

67

be achieved among driveways, patios, staircases, decks, and swimming pools. Though not without displays of colour, the aesthetic contribution of grasses is generally found in their effects upon lines and shapes, and in the multiplicity of textures and forms that they bring. In Figure 3-25 and 3-26, ornamental grasses such as Porcupine Grass (*Miscanthus sinensis* 'Strictus') and bamboo fully frame a patio, mediating between the house and the evergreen screen towering in the background. And *Calamagrostis* adds the right flavour to the ascending walk in front of the house, giving an erect movement emphasizing the upward flow. Its brown-orange spikes create the subtle focal point of the entire composition, enlightening the entire planting, complimenting the man-made structures.

Garden Design by Oehme, van Sweden & Associates, Inc.

FIGURE 3-25

Garden Design by Oehme, van Sweden & Associates, Inc.

FIGURE 3-26

Ornamental Grasses and Water

The association of grass and water is an ancient one. Moisture-loving grasses grow along the edges of ponds, their tall blades reflecting in the water, hiding the embankment and the water's depth. A mysterious call of nature cries out as the wind passes through the reeds. There are ancient memories here, and some very recent ones. Memories of walks along inlets and bays leading out to the ocean, or of the wild rice or salt-hay fields, and the papyrus of the Nile Valley. Wherever man has found water, it seems he has discovered the habitat of some form of grass, rush, or sedge.

The introduction of water into the garden has a distinguished history. The presence, even the very sound of running water is an essential element of Japanese garden style—a style that has inspired Western landscape designers to incorporate naturalized pools, ponds, streams, and waterfalls into their designs. Chinese, English, French, and Italian landscape architectural uses of water have also influenced the modern incorporation of water elements. It is with this background in mind that the incorporation of grasses into the landscape gains new dimensions. For it brings with it the associations of natural habitats. Thus the

***P**hyllostachys aurea* (Yellow Groove Bamboo) provides a stately presence in this picturesque water garden.

69

Able to withstand salt air and high winds, *Cortaderia selloana* (Pampas Grass) is an excellent grass for coastal areas.

introduction of grasses alongside the pool or stream, even alongside the formal fountain or artificially styled swimming pool, will tend to help naturalize and integrate the water element with the landscape and the natural surrounding and background for the design.

In the natural pond setting the designer aims to obscure harsh demarcation of the planting and the pond's boundary in order to achieve a gradual transition and a natural appearance. To this end it is important to soften the line of the pond. Undulated and irregularly formed obtuse arcs are well-suited to achieve this natural effect. Simple boulders or stones with rounded edges make for a more convincing coping than the more conventional cement or blue stone. The use of boulders adds rhythmic accents to the otherwise continuous line of the embankment. Large boulders give off a vertical movement, which is enhanced by their reflection in the water.

The selection of plants also determines the aesthetic quality of the boundary line. Grasses with significant height will reflect longer images, enriching the surface of the water and providing the illusion of greater depth and enlarged landscaped dimensions. The movement of grasses swaying in the wind mirrors the nature of the water itself, creating a highly satisfying aesthetic synthesis.

Garden Design by Thomas A. Reinhardt

FIGURE 3-27

Where the planting is pendular and droops over the embankment, the line is further obscured and the natural design aim gains greater force. The pendular movement bridges the two levels of surfaces: the water and the embankment.

Grasses are, in general, highly suitable for plantings along natural ponds or streams, because of their effect on the boundary line. Higher grasses create lovely patches of movement along the water's edge, bringing multiple undulations. Their irregular shapes soften the all-too-perfect curves of man-made forms, set up rhythmic accent points, and screen what lies behind (or screen part of the water's edge from a path, so as to set the stage for the dramatic discovery). Where the grass only partially screens the water, as with the case of Porcupine Grass or cat's-tail, the water penetrates through establishing a subtle background.

The mediating effect of the ornamental grass connecting the pond with a perennial bed is well illustrated in Figure 3-27. Here the *Sedum* with *Rudbeckia* 'Goldsturm' stands alongside a clump of ornamental grass. The weeping

FIGURE 3-28

blades of the ornamental grass fall into the pond, almost touching the water. The round, bulky shape of the grass establishes a natural edge, offsetting the more formal planting behind it. The shape of the ornamental grass is echoed by the planting of ornamental grasses in the distant background, integrating the pond planting with the perennial bed. Thus a difficult transition is successfully accomplished through the use of ornamental grasses. Notice, too, how the positioning of the ornamental grass and a few stones delineates an irregular embankment.

In Figure 3-28, ornamental grasses help to obscure the pond's edge. Chinese Silver Grass presents a wild, lush feeling, half concealing the water, which can still be seen through the gentle swaying of its inflorescences. So reminiscent of the reeds and wild grasses, this grass contributes greatly to the natural effect. Though indigenous to Eastern Asia, the Chinese Silver Grass has a 'local' rather than exotic feel. Its whitish silver spikes do much to enliven the blue-green background. Delicate and graceful, it reacts to gentle breezes. The blades sparkle as they reflect the light. Note, too, the ornamental grasses on the other side of the pond, helping to frame the pond and serving as mediators between the pond and the trees that fill the background.

Garden Design by Oehme, van Sweden & Associates, Inc

FIGURE 3-29

FIGURE 3-30

Though ornamental grasses are especially appropriate in the natural pond environment, they contribute important elements to formal pools as well. In the case of formal pools of regular shape—be they rectangular or circular—ornamental grasses can be used to either naturalize the formal lines and shapes, developing a synthesis of the natural and the formal, or to integrate the formal pool into the indigenous landscape. In the former case, the aim is to conceal the formal lines and shapes of the pool, either to create an aesthetic effect that blends the formal and natural pool ideals or else to simply soften the pool's formal rigidity. In the latter case, the aim is to maintain the formal nature of the pool and pool area while placing the pool in a natural context, so that it's appeal is less dominant, less artificial, and less invasive in the total landscape.

This latter aim is especially desirable when the pool is situated in a setting of outstanding natural beauty—when the environment itself is the greatest contribution to the aesthetic appeal of the landscape. Here the designer wants to hold onto the formal design of the pool without detracting from the natural beauty of the landscape. In this case, grasses serve to bring together and reconcile these conflicting demands.

In Figure 3-29, a planting of Maiden Grass and *Pennisetum* is located around a curved granite swimming pool with a blue stone coping. The ornamental grasses soften the pool's line, even to the point of concealing part of it, thereby offsetting the harsh rigidity of the formal curved line.

This same landscape taken from another perspective (Figure 3-30) illustrates the themes of integration and obscuring of harsh formality. The pool area and blue slate patio are surrounded by ornamental grasses, lavender, and Russian sage. Large established specimen clumps of *Miscanthus sinensis* 'Strictus,' *Molinia caerulea*, and *Helictotrichon sempervirens* provide a naturalized background for the formal pool and patio areas. Even though the garden is located in a beautifully scenic location, among reeds and wild grasses, the formal recreational area does not distract from the ever-present beauty of the location.

In Figure 3-31, daylilies, hosta, ferns, yucca, and ornamental grasses are combined in an informal planting around a pool with a patio and sitting area. The pool, which has already been naturalized to some extent by the introduction of water lilies, through the introduction of a variety of ornamental

Garden Design by Oehme, van Sweden & Associates, Inc.

FIGURE 3-31

grasses, gains significant natural integration. The informal planting softens the rigid, straight lines of the pool even though the planting is not situated adjacent to the pool but only in the vicinity.

Figure 3-32 is a beautiful example of the exquisite beauty of ornamental grass in its full autumn colour. Here, a lovely footbridge serves as a boundary between the planting and the water. This naturalized water garden with established woody plant specimens does not make extensive use of grasses; still, the single presence of Maiden Grass in autumn is sufficient to reveal the best reason of all for the inclusion of grasses in any pool setting: their beauty. The grasses give colour, light, texture and, a focal point for the composition.

Garden Design by Thomas A. Reinhardt

Garden Design by Thomas A. Reinhardt

FIGURE 3-32

FIGURE 3-33

Comprehensive Design with Ornamental Grasses

The preceding sections have discussed the basic principles and applications of designing with ornamental grasses: how ornamental grasses can be combined with annuals, perennials, ground covers, shrubs, trees, and other grasses to generate various aesthetic effects; how they can be used along paths, patios, driveways, and houses; and how they can enhance pools, ponds, and streams. This final section will take a look at the subject of complex and comprehensive designs—examples of how all these various adaptations of ornamental grasses can be combined and synthesized into a fully landscaped creation.

A comprehensive landscape must combine a variety of elements—some contrasting, others harmonizing—into an original work of art that is appropriate to that particular setting without being a mere imitation of a well-known style. In this section, I will develop some of the ideas pertaining to comprehensive design by analyzing two gardens that I have designed, installed, and maintained on Long Island, USA. In these gardens, ornamental grasses play a significant role, but they represent only a few motifs in a symphony of design. Set between a freshwater pond and the Atlantic Ocean, the garden in Figure 3-33 combines a variety of grasses, perennials, dwarf shrubs, and ground covers to present a tapestry of interwoven textures, colours, and shapes. Dwarf woody ornamentals combine with flowering perennials and established clumps of Maiden Grass in the middle ground on the right. The Maiden Grass, with its finely textured, pendular foliage, is fountainlike in appearance. The groups of Japanese irises planted in this garden function as grasses—their stiff, long leaves produce a grasslike effect. This is clearly illustrated in Figure 3-34, where they combine with yellow-flag irises and Chinese Silver Grass in the foreground. Ornamental grasses and flowering perennials, such as irises and daylilies, combine to bring about a natural feel and to act as mediators between the indigenous flora and the cultivated plantings.

FIGURE 3-34

Garden Design by Thomas A. Reinhardt

This allows for a rather successful integration of the garden into the environment. The informal design of perennials bordering the river round-stone path helps make the path less obtrusive. Scottish and Irish moss is planted between the stones. These mosses also have a grasslike appearance and can survive when trampled on. The various uses of foliage make this garden an attractive and exciting place even when the many varieties of perennials are not in bloom.

The vivid blue of the natural pond in the background of Figure 3-35 inspired and determined the use of foliage. Often, blue foliage was used, as we can see in the case of the low junipers, Moor Grass (*Helictotrichon sempervirens*), and other perennials, some having blue flowers. Moor Grass (*Molinia caerulea*) has a loose, airy character when its panicles appear in the flower stems, which are about double the height of the dense grass clump. It is used to harmonize with (colour), yet contrast (texture), the junipers, creating an interesting tension. It is also a good companion planting for the dwarf pines.

Another view of the garden (Figure 3-36) illustrates the use of various ground covers to integrate the stone paths. The paths can be seen as stream beds—an association that is enhanced by the ever-present body of water pulling and drawing the garden into the natural

Garden Design by Thomas A. Reinhard:

FIGURE 3-35

beauty of the location. Within this context, a subtle use of *Deschampsia* and *Pennisetum* highlights the path's division and breaks the horizontal flow of the sedum.

In another part of the garden (Figure 3-37) a sitting area has been established. The planting of rugosa rose, bayberry, flowering perennials, Ribbon Grass, and Eu-ropean Dune Grass (*Elymus arenarius*) helps to integrate the setting into its natural surrounding. Allowing the Ribbon Grass to grow into the European Dune Grass achieves a wild and unique look. The use of European Dune Grass is especially symbolic, for it calls forth the presence of the beach environment, which lies in very close proximity. In fact, on the other side of the garden, a single berm separates the pond and beach environments.

Directly beyond this border planting, another transition planting with *Elymus arenarius*, dusty miller, and American Beach Grass (Figure 3-38) fully completes the integration of the garden with its natural surrounding. With its blue-grey foliage, the European Dune Grass calls forth a relationship between the garden and the ocean in the background. The piece of driftwood works as a sculptural focal point for the composition. Placed among the beach grass it has a distinctly natural shape and feel as it marks the end of the controlled

FIGURE 3-36

Garden Design by Thomas A. Reinhardt

Garden Design by Thomas A. Reinhardt

FIGURE 3-37

FIGURE 3-38

Garden Design by Thomas A. Reinhardt

Garden Design by Thomas A. Reinhardt

garden and the beginning of the indigenous landscape.

This second example of a comprehensive design (Figure 3-39) is a garden that combines an installed pond and stream with shrubs and perennials that have been developed into a rather extensive English border. Unlike the conventional English perennial border, there is depth to the planting, enabling the introduction of paths and the creation of areas that are not immediately revealed but require exploration and penetration into the garden. The use of perennials and shrubs is also unconventional, for they are highly dynamic, changing in colour and textural patterns many times throughout

FIGURE 3-39

Garden Design by Thomas A. Reinhardt

FIGURE 3-40

FIGURE 3-41

Garden Design by Thomas A. Reinhardt

FIGURE 3-42

the year. The garden has a naturalized pond that is only partially visible from the house and lawn areas. The pond is home to aquatic plants, fish, and frogs. It is a local meeting ground for birds and bees, butterflies, and small animals.

Fundamental to this aim is the wild, lush, vital, captivating environment that is created. In this context, ornamental grasses are used not only for their naturalizing force but also for their lovely textures and aquatic associations.

From another angle (Figure 3-40), a stream enters the pond. Here, the grasses border the stream with their blades flowing over the stone edge, touching the water. There are also ornamental grasses on the other bank of the pond, which are framed by deciduous shrubs in the background.

In Figure 3-41, taken in early summer, various ornamental grasses combine with irises to help unify the garden. A wood-chip path, only partially visible in the photograph, serves as an undulating border against the lawn. In the middleground, Ribbon Grass, and European Dune Grass can be seen. In the background of the photograph, going away from the pond, Maiden Grass is visible. It is rather low in height, due to it being early in the season.

In late summer, the garden comes alive with colour (Figure 3-42). *Astilbe chinensis* 'Pumila,'

FIGURE 3-43

Caryopteris (blue shrub), black-eyed Susan (*Rudbeckia*), marsh-mallow (*Hibiscus*), joe-pye weed (*Eupatorium purpurea*), feather-poppy (*Macleaya cordata*), and Japanese irises (*Iris kaempferi*) combine with the lovely specimen planting of Maiden Grass (*Miscanthus sinensis* 'Gracillimus') to create a colourful and texturally dynamic composition. From another perspective (Figure 3-43), we get a glimpse of orange chrysanthemums in the background. The picture looks more like a wildflower meadow than a perennial bed, due to the introduction of the naturalizing foliage and the commanding presence of the *Miscanthus*.

This garden is a careful interplay of flowering perennials and wild natural textures and foliage shapes. The bold, dark foliage of *Canna* contrasts with the Ribbon Grass in the foreground (Figure 3-44). The sharply diverging perennials are at once dynamic and explosive, yet in relationship to the composition as a whole they play a well-defined and calculated role. Colour balance and textural repetitions create the necessary harmony that will not escape the trained eye. Thus, a naturalized presentation of a perennial border becomes a dynamic work of art. *Polygonum*, *Vitex*, *Sedum*, *Hosta*, *Canna*, and *Phalaris arundinacea* are the elements from which aesthetically pleasing pictures are painted.

FIGURE 3-44

A Catalogue
of Grasses

ACHNATHERUM CALAMAGROSTIS

Achnatherum calamagrostis

Common name: Silver Spike Grass

Family: Gramineae

This grass is indigenous to the Mediterranean region and the Alps. It grows in dense clumps from 2 to 2½ feet (61 to 77 centimetres) high, without running rhizomes, and has a very long decorative season. The culms are stiff and the foliage is blue-green. The 8-inch (21-centimetre) panicles appear in June and last into late autumn, changing from a shiny silver-white to a brownish yellow. This grass prefers an alkaline soil in a well-drained and sunny location.

Silver Spike Grass looks best when grown as a specimen or blended with perennials. The panicles can be used for fresh or dried arrangements.

Propagation by division.

Hardy.

Ammophila breviligulata

Common name: American Beach Grass

Family: Gramineae

This 2- to 3½-foot (62- to 107-centimetre) tall grass grows in dense clusters with deep, extensively creeping rhizomes. The grey-green leaf blades are narrow, long, tough, and involute. In late July or early August, 10-inch (25-centimetre) spikelike panicles appear. They are pale beige and have a nearly cylindrical shape.

Because of its capacity to grow in both a sandy and a salty environment, this grass is valuable for the stabilization of the soil along the coastal areas. It requires full sun and will grow through deposited sand layers.

The best time to plant American Beach Grass is when it is dormant—between October and April. Since it is not usually available with a root ball, it must be planted bareroot anytime between October and April when the ground is not frozen. Foot traffic is harmful to it because broken stems die off.

Propagation by division and seed.

Hardy.

Andropogon scoparius

(Hortus III: *Schizachyrium scoparium*)

Common name: Little Blue Stem

Family: Gramineae

This grass grows up to 2 to 3 feet (62 to 92 centimetres) high in loose clusters that branch out at the top. The leaf sheaths and blades are glabrous and are usually green, blue, or purple in colour, turning red in the autumn. The inflorescence is a silvery, 2- to 2½-inch (5- to 6-centimetre) raceme. It requires full sun and ordinary garden soil and flowers in late summer.

The Little Blue Stem can be used in mass plantings or in small groups in the perennial border. It is good in combination with late-summer flowering perennials. It is indigenous from North America to Mexico.

Propagation by division or seed.

Hardy in southwest United Kingdom.

Arrhenatherum elatius subsp. bulbosum 'Variegatum'

Common name: Bulbous Oat Grass
Family: Gramineae

The Bulbous Oat Grass from Europe grows in loose clumps from 1 to 2 feet (31 to 62 centimetres) high. It is valued for the bright white vertical margins in the centre of the blue-green grass blades. The foliage is especially attractive during the cold season of spring and autumn. New shoots start coming up in April. However, the foliage becomes less attractive over the summer, when the plant can be cut back. It flowers from early to late August, with narrow, pale green or light yellow panicles. It should be planted in moist soil enriched with organic matter, in sunny or lightly shaded areas.

It can be utilized as an accent plant, in border plantings, or in rock gardens. It is named after the subglobose internodes on the base of the stem. Propagation by division.
Hardy.

AMMOPHILA BREVILIGULATA

ARRHENATHERUM ELATIUS SUBSP. BULBOSUM 'VARIEGATUM'

91

BAMBOOS:

ARUNDINARIA PYGMAEA

Arundinaria pygmaea

Common name: Pygmy Bamboo
Family: Gramineae
Tribe: Bambuseae

The Pygmy Bamboo originates from Japan. With its 1-foot (30-centimetre) growth, it is one of the smallest bamboos. Its slender stems are bright green, with purple nodes and zigzagging 1-inch (2.5-centimetre) internodes. The bright green leaf blades are broadly lanceolate and pubescent, and grow up to 5 inches (13 centimetres) long and ¾ inch (2 centimetres) wide.

Once established through its fast-spreading rhizomes, it will survive despite dryness, shade, and root competition from trees and shrubs. It is therefore valuable as a ground cover in partially shaded woodland settings.
Hardy.

Arundinaria viridi-striata

Family: Gramineae
Tribe: Bambuseae

The slender, dark-purplish-green stems reach a height of 2 ½ to 3 feet (77 to 92 centimetres). In spring, the new leaves are golden yellow with green stripes, 7 inches (18 centimetres) long and (44 centimetres) 1 ½ inches wide, and densely hairy on the underside. The leaf blades are rounded at the base and pointed at the tip.

Though flowering is infrequent, when it does occur plants of this species flower simultaneously over a wide area. It prefers partial to full shade and needs a winter mulch in colder regions. Its native country is Japan. Propagation by division or by cuttings of underground rhizomes taken in early to late winter.
Hardy.

ARUNDINARIA VIRIDI-STRIATA

Arundinaria nitida (Syn. *Sinarundinaria nitida*)

Common name: Fountain Bamboo
Family: Gramineae
Tribe: Bambuseae

This bamboo from China is slow growing and creates large, 12-foot- (3.6-metres-) high clumps with arching stems. The rhizomes are short and therefore are not invasive. The Fountain Bamboo has a delicate foliage with narrow, linear evergreen leaves, which drop only in very cold winters. The shiny purple culms are first erect and droop slightly as they mature. The diameter of the mature stems is ¾ inch (2 centimetres).

This bamboo does well in full sun and a well-drained, average soil. Fountain Bamboo is appropriate around water gardens, as a screen or background plant, or as a specimen plant.
Propagation by division in early spring.
Hardy.

Phyllostachys aureosulcata

Common name: Yellow Groove Bamboo
Family: Gramineae
Tribe: Bambuseae

The vigorously growing Yellow Groove Bamboo comes from China and creates thick groves 10 to 30 feet (3 to 9 metres) in height when fully established. The dark green leaves are 4 to 6 inches (10 to 15 centimetres) long. The young culms are green; when mature, they turn olive green, with yellow grooves—hence its name. The mature stems are 1 ½ inches (46 centimetres) in diameter. When the young shoots first appear in spring, they are edible, and within six weeks they reach their full height for that year. The plants continue to grow rapidly for about 15 years, at which time they reach their full growth. The Yellow Groove Bamboo needs rich, moisture-retaining soil in full sun in an area protected from strong winds.

This plant has a notorious spreading habit; in order to prevent unwanted sprawl, plant the bamboo in large, bottomless containers or install in-ground barriers such as fibreglass panels. This bamboo is useful as a specimen plant, background planting, or in masses for the establishment of a bamboo grove.
Propagation of young plants by division best in late winter; older clumps are propagated by 12-inch (30-centimetre) cuttings of the rhizomes taken just before shoot growth begins in spring.
Hardy.

Arundo donax

Common name: Giant Reed
Family: Gramineae

This bold grass grows from thick rhizomes in large clumps up to 15 feet (4.5 metres) high. With its light green to grey-green linear, lanceolate, 2-ranked leaves it has a bamboo-like appearance. The leaves are 1 to 2 feet (31 to 62 centimetres) long and 2 to 3 inches (5 to 8 centimetres) wide.

The Giant Reed has greenish to purplish dense panicles up to two feet (62 centimetres) long from mid-October into the winter, but it seldom flowers in colder zones. It thrives in full sun in fertile, moist, but well-drained soil, and needs a good winter mulch in areas with colder winters. It can be used as a specimen plant, as a screen, or in background plantings. It is also appropriate for waterside landscapes. Native to Southern Europe.
Propagation by division, or cuttings taken of rhizomes during dormant phase. Tender.

ARUNDO DONAX

Bouteloua gracilis

Common name: Mosquito Grass

Family: Gramineae

This prairie grass from North America forms 1- to 2-foot (31- to 62-centimetre) high, dense clumps with narrow blades. Brown mosquito-like spikelets are horizontally attached to the erect flower stems.

Mosquito Grass likes full sun and dry soil. It is useful in naturalized areas, and its seed heads make beautiful dried flower arrangements.

Propagation by division or seed.

Hardy.

Briza maxima

Common name: Big Quaking Grass

Family: Gramineae

This annual from the Mediterranean region grows 2 feet (62 centimetres) high. Its light yellow panicles, which bloom from May to August, carry a few ovate spikelets on slender, drooping pedicels. The panicles are useful for dried arrangements.

Briza media

Common name: Quaking Grass

Family: Gramineae

This grass from Eurasia grows 6 to 18 inches (15 to 46 centimetres) high and creates dense green tufts. The inflorescence is a loose, pyramidical panicle with rattlesnake-like seed heads on erect stems above the tufts of foliage. The heart-shaped spikelets are drooping. Flowering time is May to June.

The Quaking Grass needs slightly moist soil in full sun or light shade. It should not be planted too close to more vigorous plants, because of root competition. This grass is a good rock garden plant and its panicles are valuable for dried arrangements. It can be used as well in perennial plantings.

Propagation by division or seed.

Hardy.

BRIZA MAXIMA

94

Calamagrostis x acutiflora 'Stricta'

Common name: Feather Reed Grass
Family: Gramineae

This clump-forming grass gives a strong, vertical line, with rigidly erect stems up to 5 feet (1.5 metres) high. Its slender, yellow spikes begin to appear on the flower stems in June. The bright gold colour lasts well into winter.

Feather Reed Grass grows in average garden soil, in full sun to partial shade. It combines well with woody ornamentals, and can also be used as an accent plant or in a background planting.

Propagation by division in spring.

Hardy.

Carex buchananii

Common name: Leatherleaf Sedge Grass
Family: Cyperaceae

Leatherleaf Sedge Grass originates in New Zealand and is valued for its shiny, brown-bronze foliage, which lasts almost the entire year. It grows in airy tufts, 18 to 24 inches (46 to 61 centimetres) tall with loose, weeping, narrow blades, curling at the end.

Leatherleaf Sedge Grass grows in moist soil, enriched with organic matter. It is used in rock gardens and perennial borders, in combination with other ornamental grasses (especially those with blue foliage), and in combination with woody ornamentals.

Propagation by division or seed.

Hardy.

CALAMAGROSTIS X ACUTIFLORA 'STRICTA'

Carex grayi

Common name: Gray's or Mace Sedge

Family: Cyperaceae

This clump-forming, 2- to 2½-foot (61- to 76-centimetre) high sedge is indigenous to swampy locations in North America. It is known for its attractive, green, globe-shaped seed heads, which appear from June to August. The ¼- to 1½-inch (6- to 12-millimetre) leaves stay green into late autumn.

Gray's Sedge grows in partial shade in moisture-retaining soil or shallow water and is a valuable plant for areas around ponds or streams and in naturalized plantings. It can also be used in a perennial border and for cutting. Propagation by division or seed.

Hardy.

Carex morrowii 'Aurea Variegata' ('Evergold')

Common name: Japanese Sedge Grass

Family: Cyperaceae

This clump-forming grass, 1 to 1½ feet (31 to 46 centimetres) high, comes from Japan. It is valued for its pendulous bright yellow grass blades with green vertical lines. It is evergreen and grows in clusters. The flowering stems are triangular and solid; the inconspicuous flowers barely grow taller than the foliage.

The Japanese Sedge Grass should be planted in full sun to partial shade, in acidic, moist soil rich in organic matter. It is a valuable plant for border plantings, edgings, woodland settings, rock gardens, and pond areas. Propagation by division or seed sown in the autumn.

Hardy.

CAREX MORROWII 'AUREA VARIEGATA'

Carex muskingumensis

Common name: Palm Branch Sedge

Family: Cyperaceae

This sedge, native to North America, grows in erect clumps 2 to 3 feet (62 to 92 centimetres) high, and achieves its full beauty in about 2 to 3 years. The culms carry the weeping, light green, lanceolate, leaf blades up to the tip, which resembles a small palm branch. The brown inflorescences, which are not very attractive, appear in July.

Palm Branch Sedge grows in sun to partial shade, in acidic, moisture-retaining soil enriched with organic matter. It is used in rock gardens, waterside gardens, naturalized plantings, and perennial borders.

Propagation by division or seed.

Hardy.

Carex plantaginea

Common Name: Wide Leaf Sedge

Family: Cyperaceae

Wide Leaf Sedge, native to North America, is named after its ¾ - to 1-inch (2- to 3-centimetre) wide evergreen leaves, which form attractive 6- to 12-inch (15- to 31-centimetre) high clumps. It produces yellow, 8-inch (20-centimetre) inflorescences from April to May.

This grass should be planted in partial to full shade in soil that is rich in organic matter. Wide Leaf Sedge is a valuable ground cover for woodland settings and for shaded areas of a rock garden.

Propagation by division or seed.

Hardy.

CAREX MUSKINGUMENSIS

CORTADERIA SELLOANA

Cortaderia selloana

Common name: Pampas Grass
Family: Gramineae

Pampas Grass, king of the ornamental grasses, is native to Brazil, Argentina, and Chile. It grows 8 to 12 feet (21 to 31 centimetres) high, in large upright clumps, and is used in gardens because of its showy feathery panicles, which are 1 to 2 feet (31 to 62 centimetres) long. The flowers range from silvery white to pink and last from late September to late October.

Pampas Grass has to be planted in full sun in fertile, well-drained soil, and should receive adequate moisture and fertilizer in the spring only. It cannot take undrained locations, especially in the winter. In areas with cold winters, the clumps should be tied up and the root area should receive a good mulch.

It can be used at the back of perennial borders or as screens. The panicles make elegant cut flowers for fresh and dried arrangements.
Propagation by division.
Tender.

Cymbopogon citratus

Common name: Lemon Grass
Family: Gramineae

Lemon Grass, which is indigenous to southern India and Ceylon, has been cultivated in Florida for the lemon-grass oil. It grows in dense clumps, up to 6 feet (1.8 metres) high, the tallest of the slender branches drooping slightly. The leaf blades are up to 3 feet (92 centimetres) long and ½ inch (1.2 centimetres) wide, tapered at both ends, with scabrous margins. Lemon Grass rarely flowers.
Propagation by division.
Tender.

Dactylis glomerata "Variegata"

Common Name: Variegated Cocksfoot
Family: Gramineae

This grass, native to Eurasia, is commonly cultivated for meadows and pastures. Its cultivar 'Variegata' is valued for its beautiful, vertical, green and white variegated foliage, which creates dense 1- to 2-foot (31- to 62-centimetres) tall tufts. It is very attractive from early spring through early summer. The flowers, however, are not of decorative value; remove the seed heads to avoid reseeding.

Variegated Cocksfoot needs average soil and does well in full sun or partial shade. It is useful as an edging, accent, or specimen plant.
Propagation by division.
Hardy.

CYMBOPOGON CITRATUS

Deschampsia caespitosa
Common name: Tufted Hair Grass
Family: Gramineae

Tufted Hair Grass is indigenous to the Northern Hemisphere. It is valued for its pale green or purple-tinged airy panicles, which appear in masses in late June and last through late August. The dark green foliage grows in dense clumps about 1½ to 2 feet (46 to 62 centimetres) high and is attractive through most of the year.

This ornamental grass prefers acidic, moist soil and a sunny or partially shaded location. It is a good plant for the partially shaded woodland, and can also be used in the mixed perennial border or as an accent plant. The panicles are good for fresh or dried arrangements.

Propagation by division or seed.

Hardy.

DESCHAMPSIA

Elymus arenarius

Common Name: Blue Lyme Grass

Family: Gramineae

Blue Lyme Grass is a valuable seashore plant because of its rampant, rhizomatous growth that prevents erosion. This coarsely textured grass has a light blue, glaucous foliage and grows to a height of 1½ to 2 feet (47 to 62 centimetres). The beige flower spikes are slender but bristly and appear sporadically. It likes full sun and very sandy soil.

This ornamental grass is appropriate for dune plantings, but can also work well in perennial borders. Since it is invasive, plant Blue Lyme Grass in bottomless, plastic containers when set near other plants.

Propagation by division.

Hardy.

Eragrostis trichodes

Common name: Sand Love Grass

Family: Gramineae

The Sand Love Grass plant grows in erect clusters up to 4 feet (1.2 metres) high. It has dark green foliage, with long, slightly arching leaf blades. The long and airy panicles appear in July and last until late summer.

It thrives in light sandy soil in a full sunny location, and is a useful specimen plant and can also be planted in a group in a mixed perennial border. The panicles are good for cutting.

Propagation by division or seed.

Hardy.

ERIANTHUS RAVENNAE

100

Erianthus ravennae

Common name: Ravenna Grass
Family: Gramineae

In areas with cold winters, where Pampas Grass is not hardy enough to survive, one might want to try Ravenna Grass instead. It has a tall, stately appearance and is between 4 and 6 feet (1 to 2 metres) high when fully grown. The stems are stout, with long, narrow leaf blades. In the autumn, the plant turns brown with tinges of orange or purple. From late September to late October, 1- to 2-foot (31-to 63-centimetre) long silver-white panicles appear. Flowering might be limited if there is an early frost.

Ravenna Grass, which is a good plant for the back of the perennial border, for screen plantings, or as a specimen, is indigenous to Southern Europe and should be planted in moist but well-drained fertile soil.

Propagation by division or seed.

Hardy in the southern United Kingdom.

Festuca amethystina

Common Name: Amethyst Blue Fescue
Family: Gramineae

This Fescue grass is indigenous to the Central and Southeast Europe. It forms 12- inch (31-centimetre) tall, finely textured mounds. The evergreen foliage is dark blue-green and filiform. In May, narrow, 4-inch (10-centimetre) panicles appear on 20-inch (51-centimetre) culms.

Amethyst Blue Fescue requires full sun and a sandy soil enriched with organic matter. It makes a handsome ground cover in sunny locations.

Propagation by division.

Hardy.

FESTUCA GLAUCA

Festuca glauca

Common name: Blue Fescue
Family: Gramineae

Blue Fescue is valued for its dense evergreen tufts of silvery blue foliage. It grows from ½ to 1 foot (15 to 31 centimetres) tall, and has slender, involute leaf blades. From early June to early July, finely textured greenish beige panicles appear. They should be removed after flowering in order to strengthen the plants.

Blue Fescue needs light, well-drained soil and full sun. It grows best in cooler climates and should be divided every 2 to 3 years. Species *Festuca ovina* is cultivated as a pasture or meadow grass. Blue Fescue can be used in ground-cover plantings, as an accent or in small groups in the perennial border, in the rock garden, or as an edging plant. It can also be combined with dwarf woody ornamentals.

Propagation by division.

Hardy.

Festuca mairei

Common Name: Maires Fescue

Family: Gramineae

The Maires Fescue has a coarser texture than other Fescue species. It is indigenous to Morocco and grows in dense clumps 2 feet (62 centimetres) high. The leaf blades are grey-green and have sharp margins. In spring, slender panicles appear on stiff culms that grow to 3 or 4 feet (92 to 122 centimetres).

This grass needs a well-drained soil enriched with organic matter and a sunny location. Maires Fescue is a good accent plant when combined with perennials or low woody ornamentals. It can also be planted in clusters. Propagation by division or seed.

Hardy.

FESTUCA MAIREI

Glyceria maxima 'Variegata'

Common name: Reed Sweet Grass

Family: Gramineae

Reed Sweet Grass is indigenous to Europe and the temperate regions of Asia and North America. It grows about 2 feet (62 centimetres) tall and its main decorative feature is its foliage which is creamy yellow with green vertical variegation. The blooming time is July to August; the inflorescence is a brownish panicle with flattened spikelets.

This grass has to be cultivated in fertile, moist to wet soil, rich in organic matter. It can take a water level up to 8 inches (20 centimetres). This grass is strongly rhizomatous; unless used as an extensive ground cover, it should be planted in a submerged bottomless plastic container to avoid spreading into neighbouring plants.

Reed Sweet Grass makes a good accent plant in a water garden, at the edge of a pond, or in shallow water, where it can be planted en masse. Propagation by division or cuttings from rhizomes.

Hardy.

Hakonechloa macra 'Aureola'

Family: Gramineae

This grass was recently introduced into this country from Japan. It grows from ½ to 1½ feet (15 to 46 centimetres) high and has a strongly arching habit as it turns to seek the light. The soft foliage is bright yellow with fine green stripes; the flower is inconspicuous. This grass is slightly rhizomatous but does not become invasive.

Hakonechloa macra is grown in fertile, well-drained soil rich in organic matter, in partial to full shade. This is a fine plant for the woodland, where it can be planted as a specimen or accent plant or in groups. It also makes an attractive edging plant.

Propagation by division.

Hardy.

HELICTOTRICHON SEMPERVIRENS

HAKONECHLOA MACRA 'AUREOLA'

Helictotrichon sempervirens

Common name: Blue Oat Grass

Family: Gramineae

Blue Oat Grass, indigenous to Europe, forms tufted clumps about 1½ to 2½ feet (46 to 77 centimetres) high. Its stiff involute leaf blades are glaucous in colour and arch downward. From June to August, 6-inch (15-centimetre) beige panicles stand on 5-foot- (1.5-metre-) high culms. The panicles seem to "float" above the evergreen foliage.

Blue Oat Grass needs full sun and a well-drained soil rich in organic matter. It is an excellent plant for the rock garden and the perennial border, where it can be planted in small groups or as an accent plant. It also combines well with woody ornamentals.

Propagation by division or seed.

Hardy.

103

Holcus mollis 'Variegatus'

Common Name: Variegated Creeping Soft Grass
Family: Gramineae

This grass is indigenous to Europe and is occasionally cultivated as a meadow grass. It grows from 6 to 12 inches (15 to 31 centimetres) high. Its aesthetic contribution to gardens lies in its velvety, pubescent, white-striped, green foliage, which spreads out to form a carpet. Light green, villous panicles appear in June and continue into August.

This variegated grass should be planted in light, sandy soil in full sun to partial shade. It can be incorporated into the perennial border and can be used in the rock garden. It is appropriate as both an edging plant and a ground cover. Because of its strong, rhizomatous growth, precautions must be taken to keep it from crowding out other plants.
Propagation by division.
Hardy.

Hordeum jubatum

Common name: Fox-tail Barley
Family: Gramineae

This ornamental grass is indigenous to the temperate Northern Hemisphere. It grows in upright tufts of green scabrous foliage from 2 to 2 ½ feet (30 to 77 centimetres) high. Its main value lies in its drooping 4-inch- (10-centimetre-) long spikes, which are purple or green. The tips are dense with awns that grow up to 3 inches (8 centimetres) long. Blooming time is from early June to early July. Fox-tail Barley needs an average garden soil in full sun. It loses its attractiveness shortly after bloom and should therefore be cut back in mid-August.

This grass can be utilized as a cut flower and can be planted in perennial borders or naturalized plantings. When used as a cut flower, the spikes should be harvested before fully matured. Fox-tail Barley is generally grown as an annual, in the United Kingdom.
Propagation by seed.
Hardy.

HORDEUM JUBATUM

Hystrix patula

Common Name: Bottlebrush Grass
Family: Gramineae

This grass, indigenous to North America, is named after its dense, 2 ½ - inch (6-centimetre) awned spikes, which resemble a bottle brush. The spikes grow 5 to 8 inches (13 to 20 centimetres) long and turn from light green to brown. They come up in abundance in June and stay attractive into autumn. Bottlebrush grows up to 3 or 4 feet (92 to 122 centimetres) tall in an upright, open clump. The flower stems are erect and carry green leaves.

This self-seeding, short-lived, ornamental grass needs a sandy, well-drained soil enriched with organic matter in full sun to partial shade. Bottlebrush spikes are good for cutting for use in fresh or dried arrangements; they should be harvested before fully matured. This grass can be used in the perennial border and in naturalized plantings.

Propagation by division or seed.

Hardy.

Imperata cylindrica 'Red Baron'

Common name: Japanese Blood Grass
Family: Gramineae

The main attraction of this plant from Japan lies in its brilliant foliage. Though the leaf base is green, the rest of the plant is blood red, and the colour lasts throughout the growing season. This slow-growing grass is rhizomatous and has an upright open habit 1 to 1 ½ feet (31 to 46 centimetres) tall. It grows best in partial shade in moist but well-drained soil.

This ornamental grass makes a beautiful accent plant, and is an attractive ground cover in a partially shaded woodland location.

Propagation by division.

Tender.

IMPERATA CYLINDRICA 'RED BARON'

Juncus effusus

Common name: Common Rush

Family: Juncaceae

This rush is extensively grown in Japan for weaving tatami, the standard floor covering in Japanese homes. It grows 1 to 3 feet (31 to 92 centimetres) high and has a rigid, upright appearance. The spiky stems, which are glabrous and dark green, form dense tussocks. The inconspicuous flower is yellowish green to pale brown.

The Common Rush is a moisture loving plant. It grows in water up to 8 inches (20 centimetres) deep in sun or shade, so it is ideal for the edges of ponds or streams It is native to all parts of the world in moist to wet locations. The cultivar 'Spiralis' has spirallike, twisted stems. The cultivar 'Zebrinus' has stems with white or greenish white horizontal variegation.

Propagation by division or seed.

Hardy.

Koeleria macrantha

Common name: Crested Hair Grass

Family: Gramineae

This grass grows in clumps up to 1 foot (31 centimetres) tall. It has narrow, grey-green, often involute leaf blades. Dense, glossy, spikelike panicles come up in May; they are greenish in colour. The spikelets are flattened.

Koeleria macrantha needs a well-drained, alkaline garden soil in full sun. If the soil is too fertile, the plants become short-lived. *Koeleria macrantha* looks good in mass plantings or in clusters.

Propagation by division or seed.

Hardy.

KOELERIA MACRANTHA

Luzula sylvatica

Common name: Greater Wood Rush
Family: Juncaceae

Greater Wood Rush is a sturdy, stoloniferous plant 1 foot (31 centimetres) high, which forms erect tussocks when established. The evergreen foliage is shiny, dark green, and hairy. It flowers in loose-terminal, rusty brown cymes up to 3 feet (92 centimetres) tall. Flowering time is April to May.

Greater Wood Rush is indigenous to the area from Western and Southern Europe to Caucasus. It requires a moist soil enriched with humus, in partial shade to full shade, and makes an excellent ground cover in the woodland or wild garden.
Propagation by division or seed.
Hardy.

Melica ciliata

Common name: Silky-Spike Melic Grass
Family: Gramineae

Silky-Spike Melic Grass, native to Europe, North Africa, and the Caucasus, forms clumps between 1 and 2 feet (31 and 62 centimetres) high. It has grey-green, loose foliage with mostly involute leaf blades. It flowers from mid May into June—the spikelike silky panicles turn from whitish to pale yellow when fully mature.

This grass prefers full sun in a well-drained, alkaline, sandy soil. It can be planted in groups or en masse; it makes a good naturalized planting. The panicles are appropriate for flower arrangements.
Propagation by division or seed.
Hardy.

MISCANTHUS FLORIDUS (LEFT) AND *PENNISETUM ALOPECUROIDES* (RIGHT)

Miscanthus floridulus

Common name: Giant Chinese Silver Grass
Family: Gramineae

Giant Chinese Silver Grass is indigenous to Japan and the Pacific Islands. It grows in erect clumps 8 to 10 feet (2.4 to 3 metres) high. Its pale, glaucous-green linear leaves (1 ¼ inches [3.2 centimetres] wide and up to 2 ½ feet [77 centimetres] long) arch downward. Its white panicles form a pyramid shape up to 20 inches (51 centimetres) long, with awned lemmas. This *Miscanthus* species does not flower in colder regions, but it is still worthwhile to use because of its striking appearance and size.

Giant Chinese Silver Grass needs full sun to partial shade in soil enriched with organic matter. It needs adequate moisture. Since it can take some root competition from trees and shrubs, there are many possibilities for placement in the landscape, especially in combination with woody ornamentals. This grass works well as a specimen, a background or screen plant, or as a skeleton for a larger perennial border.
Propagation by division.
Hardy.

107

Miscanthus sacchariflorus

Common name: Silver Banner Grass
Family: Gramineae

Silver Banner Grass, indigenous to Asia, grows in upright clumps, 5 to 7 feet (1.5 to 2 metres) high. It has erect stiff culms and is rhizomatous. The green, linear leaf blades are ¾ inch (2 centimetres) wide. In early August, cone-shaped panicles, silvery white and 7 to 10 inches (18 to 25 centimetres) long, begin to appear. The grey-brown spikelets are surrounded by silky hairs, which are about twice as long as the spikelets.

Silver Banner Grass should be cultivated in light, sandy soil in full sun. It makes a good accent or specimen plant at the edge of a pond or a stream and can be used in naturalized plantings. The panicles are good for cutting.

The cultivar 'Robustus' of *Miscanthus sacchariflorus* flowers later than the species; but, unlike the species, the flowers of 'Robustus' last into the winter. Propagation by division.

Hardy in southern Europe

Miscanthus sinensis

Common name: Chinese Silver Grass
Family: Gramineae

Chinese Silver Grass is indigenous to Eastern Asia. It grows in heavy, upright, widely arching clumps 6 to 10 feet (1.8 to 3 metres) high. Leaf blades are 3½ feet (1 metre) long and ⅜ of an inch (1 centimetre) wide, green in colour, and sharply pointed at the tip. In September, long feathery panicles appear, which are silvery to pale pink.

This ornamental grass will grow in full sun to partial shade in good garden soil. However, if it is grown in a location with soil that is too high in nitrogen or too shady, the grass clumps might fall apart and require staking. The panicles are good for cutting. This grass works well as a screen, background, or specimen plant, or combined with perennials. It also is good for waterside plantings or around sitting areas in the garden. The dormant clump is attractive in the winter. Many cultivars of this species are offered on the market; a few are introduced in the following pages. Propagation by division.
Hardy.

MISCANTHUS SINENSIS 'GRACILLIMUS'

Miscanthus sinensis 'Gracillimus'

Common name: Maiden Grass
Family: Gramineae

This cultivar has a very finely textured foliage—the leaf blades are less than ¼ inch (6 millimetres) wide. They are strongly channeled and show a silvery midrib. The growing habit is upright and strongly arching. This cultivar grows from 4 to 7 feet (1.2 to 2.1 metres) high—not as tall as the species, *Miscanthus sinensis*.
Propagation by division.
Hardy.

Miscanthus sinensis 'Silberfeder'

Common name: Silverfeather Grass
Family: Gramineae

The cultivar 'Silberfeder' has showy white feathery plumes, from which it derives its name. The flower appears from late summer to late autumn. Soil and exposure requirements are similar to those of the species.
Propagation by division.
Hardy.

Miscanthus sinensis 'Strictus'

Common name: Porcupine Grass
Family: Gramineae

The spiky foliage of Porcupine Grass exhibits yellow bands similar to those of zebra grass. However, it has a more dense, upright, and stiff growing habit and greater winter hardiness than Zebra Grass.
Propagation by division.
Hardy.

MISCANTHUS SINENSIS 'STRICTUS'

MISCANTHUS SINENSIS 'VARIEGATUS'

Miscanthus sinensis 'Variegatus'

Common name: Striped Eulalia Grass
Family: Gramineae

Striped Eulalia Grass grows in upright open clumps to a height of 4 to 6 feet (1.2 to 1.8 metres). Its characteristic features are the yellow, green, and white vertically striped blades. In late September to October, it flowers in pale pink panicles that turn beige. Its soil and exposure requirements are similar to the species.

This grass can be well incorporated in the middle or background of perennial borders or it can be planted as a specimen. It works well in waterside gardens around a pond or along a stream. The panicles can be used for cutting.
Propagation by division.
Hardy.

Miscanthus sinensis 'Zebrinus'

Common name: Zebra Grass
Family: Gramineae

Zebra Grass grows in upright narrow clumps up to 7 feet (2.1 metres) high. Its common name derives from the way its arching green leaf blades are banded with white or yellow. The foliage turns buff-coloured with rusty-orange tips in the winter. From mid-September to mid-October, pale yellow to beige flowers appear. Culture requirements are like the species.

This ornamental grass can be used in the background of a perennial border, as a specimen, or in groups. It is a good plant for waterside gardens or around a pond or stream. The panicles of Zebra Grass are good for cutting.
Propagation by division.
Hardy.

MISCANTHUS SINENSIS 'VARIEGATUS'

111

MOLINIA CAERULEA

Molinia caerulea
Common name: Purple Moor Grass
Family: Gramineae

Indigenous to Eurasia, Moor Grass grows in upright arching tufts. The stems reach a height of about 3 feet (92 centimetres), the foliage about 1 to 1½ feet (31 to 46 centimetres). The dark bluish green leaf blades are soft and narrow and taper to a fine point. From July to September, 8-inch- (21-centimetre-) high delicate panicles, dark brown to purplish in colour, are in bloom. In autumn, the foliage changes to yellow and reddish-brown, but with the first frosts the grass becomes dormant and loses its attractive appearance.

Moor Grass requires acidic, moist soil that is enriched with organic matter. It can be planted in full sun or partial shade. Moor Grass looks good in naturalized plantings, combined with perennials, or as an accent plant. The panicles are good for cutting. The cultivar 'Variegata' has white and green variegated foliage; the advantage of this cultivar is that it remains attractive later into autumn than most of the species.
Propagation by division and seed.
Hardy.

Panicum virgatum
Common name: Switch Grass
Family: Gramineae

Switch Grass is indigenous to mid and eastern North America. Its sturdy, narrow, upright clumps, 3 to 5 feet (92 centimetres to 1.5 metres) high, create a strong vertical line. Leaf blades are long and narrow with rough margins. Switch Grass is known for its attractive golden-orange autumn colour. Buff brown 20-inch (51-centimetre) panicles appear in masses just above the foliage clump in late July and persist into early September. The seed heads are attractive into the winter. Switch Grass needs a fertile, well-drained soil in full sun to partial shade. It can be use for naturalized plantings or in combination with perennials. The panicles are attractive for cutting.

After becoming established for several years in the same location, Switch Grass loses its upright habit; the stems bend and the plant begins to fall apart. This does not happen to some cultivars—e.g. the cultivar 'Rotstrahlbusch,' which keeps its upright appearance.
Propagation by division or seed.
Hardy.

Pennisetum alopecuroides
Common name: Australian Fountain Grass
Family: Gramineae

Australian Fountain Grass, native to Australia, grows in mounds 3 to 4 feet (90 centimetres to 1.2 metres) tall. The bright-green narrow leaf blades are arching; the foliage provides showy autumn colour.

The spikelike, plumy panicles are 4 to 5 inches (10 to 13 centimetres) long and 2 inches (5 centimetres) in diameter, carrying bristles on each spikelet. The colour of the panicles is silvery brown. Fountain Grass flowers profusely from late August to October, and stays attractive until winter.

This grass prefers full sun and fertile soil with adequate moisture. It is necessary to divide the plants every 5 to 6 years to avoid the dying-off in the centre and to guarantee profuse flowering. The Australian Fountain Grass works very well in combination with other autumn-flowering grasses or perennials. It can be used as a specimen or accent plant or incorporated in a waterside garden.
Propagation by division.
Hardy.

Pennisetum orientale
Common name: Oriental Fountain Grass
Family: Gramineae

Oriental Fountain Grass is indigenous to Middle Asia and the Caucasus. It grows 2 to 2½ feet (62 to 77 centimetres) high in slightly open clumps. The foliage is gray-green. The panicles of the Oriental Fountain Grass are similar to those of the Australian Fountain Grass except that the panicles of the Oriental Fountain Grass are purplish in colour and bloom earlier—late June to October.

Oriental Fountain Grass grows in full sun, in well-drained sandy soil that has been enriched with organic matter. This grass can be used in ways similar to the Australian Fountain Grass.
Propagation by division or seed.
Hardy in southwest England.

Pennisetum setaceum

Common name: Crimson Fountain Grass
Family: Gramineae

Crimson Fountain Grass, indigenous to Africa, grows in gracefully arching 2- to 3-foot- (62- to 92-centimetre-) tall mounds. It has a fine texture and narrow green leaf blades. It flowers in spikelike 9-to-12-inch (23-to-31-centimetre) panicles that are pink or purple and have a nodding habit. They appear profusely in late June and persist into early October.

This ornamental grass grows in full sun to partial shade in ordinary garden soil. It can be utilized in annual or perennial borders and works well as an accent plant. The flowers are good for cutting.

Propagation by seed.

Tender.

PENNISETUM VILLOSUM

PENNISETUM SETACEUM

Pennisetum villosum

Common name: Feather Top
Family: Gramineae

This ornamental grass, indigenous to Africa, creates 1 ½ - to 2 ½ -foot- (46- to 76-centimetre-) tall mounds. The foliage is green. Flowers appear from August to late September. The 3- to 5-inch (8- to 13-centimetre) spikes are light green or white at first, changing to tawny as they age.

Feather Top should be grown in fertile soil with adequate moisture, in full sun to partial shade. It works well in annual or perennial borders. The inflorescences of this ornamental grass are attractive in dried or fresh cut flower arrangements.

Propagation by seed.

Tender.

Phalaris arundinacea 'Picta'
Common name: Ribbon Grass or Gardener's Garters
Family: Gramineae

Phalaris arundinacea is indigenous to the Northern Temperate Zone. The most decorative features of Ribbon Grass are the ¾-inch- (2- centimetre-) wide leaf blades, which are bright green with vertical white variegation. It is strongly rhizomatous and should therefore be given a large space in the garden or planted in submerged bottomless containers to keep growth under control. The flowers consist of narrow panicles 4 to 6 inches (10 to 15 centimetres) long, ranging from off-white to pink. Blooming time is early June to July.

Ribbon Grass grows in full sun to partial shade in ordinary garden soil; it will not thrive in heavy clay soil. It makes a very good ground cover and can be used successfully for soil stabilization. Ribbon Grass can be planted in perennial borders and in waterside plantings. It also stands up well to seashore conditions.

When Ribbon Grass becomes leggy and brown during the summer, it is advisable to cut the plants back to a height of 6 to 12 inches (15 to 31 centimetres). Provide liquid fertilizer and adequate water after cutting back and in a short time the plants will reproduce new growth and a fresh, attractive appearance that will last until frost.

Propagation by division.

Hardy.

PHALARIS ARUNDINACEA 'PICTA'

115

Poa chaixii
Common name: Broad-leaved Meadow Grass
Family: Gramineae

Broad-leaved Meadow Grass is indigenous to woodland glades in Central and Southern Europe. Its bright green foliage consists of leaf blades, between ¼ and ½ inch (.6 and 1.2 centimetres) wide, that end in a boat-shaped tip. In June and July, 10-inch (29-centimetre) green panicles appear in a pyramid shape. They droop slightly from the tips of 3-foot (91-centimetre) stems.

Broad-leaved Meadow Grass needs a partially shaded location and a soil enriched with leaf compost. This clump-forming grass can handle varying soil moisture. It works well in naturalized plantings in a woodland setting and can be planted en masse or in groups.

Some members of the genus *Poa* are used for forage cultivation; others are used in lawns.

Propagation by division or seed.

Hardy.

Sesleria autumnalis
Common name: Autumn Moor Grass
Family: Gramineae

Autumn Moor Grass is indigenous to an area from Northern and Eastern Italy to Albania. It grows in 1- to 1½-foot- (31- to 46-centimetre-) high clumps; it has narrow, light green leaves with scabrous margins. From September to late October narrow, spikelike panicles appear. The colour ranges from silvery-white to light brown when mature. The flower stems carry 1½- to-3-inch (4- to 8-centimetre) long leaves in the upper half, and the flowers are about 4 inches (10 centimetres) taller than the foliage mound.

This grass prefers alkaline soil in full sun to light shade. It is attractive in combination with perennials that bloom in late summer and autumn. It also works well in a border planting in front of shrubbery or wooded areas.

Propagation by division or seed.

Hardy.

Spartina pectinata 'Aureo-Marginata'
Common name: Cord Grass
Family: Gramineae

Cord Grass is indigenous to the cool temperate zones of North America. It grows in upright, arching, 4- to 8-foot (1.2- to 2.4-metre) clumps. Although it has a coarse appearance and is rhizomatous it can be kept under control. The long leaves are shiny green with yellow marginal stripes; the leaf margins are scabrous. The inflorescence appears from late August to late September and is formed by several flattened spikes on an axis which is 6 to 15 inches (15 to 38 centimetres) long. The colour changes from light yellow-beige to bright yellow in the late autumn.

Cord Grass is cultivated in full sun to partial shade and should be planted in soil enriched with organic matter.

This plant can take seashore conditions. It can be used in plantings around ponds or streams. It is a good addition to naturalized plantings, perennial borders, and as an accent plant. The flowers are excellent for cutting.

Spodiopogon sibiricus
Family: Gramineae

This ornamental grass is indigenous to Siberia, Northern China, Korea, and Japan. It has a stiff, erect appearance and grows in clumps between 4 and 5 feet (1.2 and 1.5 metres) high. The leaf blades develop a reddish tinge. The inflorescence is an airy panicle with shiny purple spikelets, which blooms from July to September.

Spodiopogon sibiricus is cultivated in fertile, well-drained soil in full sun to partial shade. It makes a good specimen plant and can also be effective in grouped plantings.

Propagation by division or seed.

Hardy.

UNIOLA LATIFOLIA

Uniola latifolia (Syn. *Chasmanthium latifolium*)

Common name: Northern Sea Oats
Family: Gramineae

This grass is indigenous to the middle and southeastern areas of North America. It grows in loose upright clumps from 3 to 4 feet (92 centimetres to 1.2 metres) high, and is rhizomatous. The light green leaf blades are broadly lanceolate and about 9 inches (23 centimetres) long. The inflorescence is an open panicle, about 10 to 12 inches (26 to 31 centimetres) long, with nodding seed heads that are at first dark green to purplish and later bronze. Spikelets are flattened. These colourful panicles stay attractive from late July, when they first appear, into the winter.

Northern Sea Oats should be cultivated in damp, fertile, well-drained soil enriched with organic matter, in full sun to partial shade. They can be used in perennial borders, waterside plantings, or naturalized areas. They also make a good accent plant and are attractive in cut-flower arrangements.

Propagation by division or seed.

Hardy.

CHASMANTHIUM LATIFOLIUM

117

APPENDIX

GROUND-COVER PLANTINGS
Arundinaria pumila
Arundinaria pygmaea
Carex morrowii 'Aurea-Variegata'
Carex plantaginea
Dactylis glomerata 'Variegata'
Deschampsia caespitosa and cultivars
Elymus arenarius
Festuca species
Glyceria maxima 'Variegata'
Helictotrichon sempervirens
Luzula sylvatica
Miscanthus sacchariflorus
Pennisetum species
Phalaris arundinacea 'Picta'
Sesleria autumnalis

SPECIMEN PLANTINGS
Arundo donax
Calamagrostis x acutiflora 'Stricta'
Cortaderia selloana
Erianthus ravennae
Festuca mairei
Helictotrichon sempervirens
Miscanthus floridulus
Miscanthus sinensis 'Gracillimus'

Miscanthus sinensis 'Silberfeder'
Miscanthus sinensis 'Strictus'
Miscanthus sinensis 'Variegatus' and other cultivars
Molinia caerulea
Panicum virgatum and cultivars
Pennisetum alopecuroides
Sinarundinaria nitida
Spartina pectinata 'Aureo-Marginata'

GRASSES FOR THE ROCK GARDEN
Arrhenatherum elatius subsp. bulbosum 'Variegatum'
Bouteloua gracilis
Briza media
Carex species and cultivars
Festuca species and cultivars
Hakonechloa macra 'Aureola'
Helictotrichon sempervirens
Holcus lanatus 'Variegatus'
Imperata cylindrica 'Red Baron'
Juncus effusus 'Spiralis'
Koeleria macrantha
Luzula species
Melica ciliata
Molinia caerulea
Sesleria species

GRASSES FOR THE WILD OR NATURAL GARDEN
Bouteloua gracilis
Briza media
Cortaderia selloana
Elymus arenarius
Festuca amethystina
Festuca mairei
Festuca ovina and cultivars
Helictotrichon sempervirens
Melica ciliata
Panicum virgatum

GRASSES FOR THE WOODLAND GARDEN
Carex species
Hystrix patula
Hakonechloa macra 'Aureola'
Imperata cylindrica 'Red Baron'
Deschampsia caespitosa and cultivars
Luzula species
Poa chaixii
Uniola latifolia (Syn. Chasmanthium latifolium)

GRASSES FOR COASTAL GARDENS
Ammophila breviligulata
Elymus arenarius
Festuca species and cultivars
Helictotrichon sempervirens
Panicum virgatum and cultivars
Phalaris arundinacea 'Picta'
Phragmites australis
Spartina pectinata 'Aureo-Marginata'

GRASSES FOR THE EDGE OF PONDS, SHALLOW WATER, AND BOGS
Arundo donax
Cyperus species
Glyceria maxima 'Variegata'
Juncus effusus and cultivars
Miscanthus sinensis and cultivars
Phalaris arundinacea 'Picta'
Phragmites australis
Spartina pectinata 'Aureo-Marginata'
Carex grayi

GRASSES FOR THE PERENNIAL BORDER
Calamagrostis x acutiflora 'Stricta'

Arrhenatherum elatius subsp. bulbosum 'Variegatum'
Arundo donax
Carex species and cultivars
Dactylis glomerata 'Variegata'
Hakonechloa macra 'Aureola'
Helictotrichon sempervirens
Imperata cylindrica 'Red Baron'
Miscanthus species and cultivars
Molinia caerulea
Panicum virgatum and cultivars
Pennisetum alopecuroides and other species and cultivars
Spartina pectinata 'Aureo-Marginata'
Uniola latifolia (Syn. Chasmanthium latifolium)

GRASSES WITH STRONG VERTICAL LINE
Arundo donax
Calamagrostis x acutiflora 'Stricta'
Cortaderia selloana
Erianthus ravennae
Juncus effusus
Miscanthus floridulus
Miscanthus sacchariflorus
Miscanthus sinensis 'Silberfeder'
Miscanthus sinensis 'Strictus'
Panicum virgatum and cultivars
Phragmites australis
Spodiopogon sibiricus

GRASSES WITH PENDULOUS WEEPING SHAPE
Deschampsia caespitosa and cultivars
Helictotrichon sempervirens
Miscanthus sinensis 'Gracillimus'
Pennisetum species
Sinarundinaria nitida
Spartina pectinata 'Aureo-Marginata'

MOUND-FORMING GRASSES
Arrhenatherum elatius subsp. bulbosum 'Variegatum'
Carex plantaginea
Festuca species
Koeleria macrantha
Luzula sylvatica
Sesleria species

GRASSES WITH VARIEGATION
Arrhenatherum elatius subsp. bulbosum 'Variegatum'
Arundo donax 'Variegata'
Carex morrowii 'Aurea Variegata'
Dactylis glomerata 'Variegata'
Glyceria maxima 'Variegata'
Hakonechloa macra 'Aureola'
Holcus lanatus 'Variegatus'
Miscanthus sinensis 'Strictus'
Miscanthus sinensis 'Variegatus'
Miscanthus sinensis 'Zebrinus'
Molinia caerulea 'Variegata'

Phalaris arundinacea 'Picta'
Spartina pectinata 'Aureo-Marginata'

GRASSES WITH BLUE FOLIAGE
Elymus arenarius
Festuca amethystina and cultivars
Festuca glauca
Helictotrichon sempervirens

GRASS WITH RED FOLIAGE
Imperata cylindrica and cultivars

EVERGREEN AND WINTERGREEN GRASSES
Carex morrowii 'Aurea Variegata'
Carex plantaginea
Deschampsia caespitosa and cultivars
Helictotrichon sempervirens

GRASSES WITH A NICE AUTUMN COLOUR
Calamagrostis species and cultivars
Miscanthus floridulus
Miscanthus sacchariflorus
Miscanthus sinensis Gracillimus'
Miscanthus sinensis purpurascens
Miscanthus sinensis 'Silberfeder'
Molinia caerulea and cultivars
Panicum virgatum and cultivars
Spodiopogon sibiricus

GRASSES WITH A SPREADING HABIT
These grasses require a lot of space because they are invasive and can take over other plantings. To avoid this problem, install a fibreglass barrier in the ground at root level. Very often, however, the spreading habitat of plants is desired for aesthetic reasons or for erosion control.
Arundinaria pumila
Arundinaria pygmaea
Elymus arenarius
Glyceria maxima 'Variegata'
Miscanthus sacchariflorus
Phalaris arundinacea 'Picta'
Phragmites australis
Spartina pectinata 'Aureo-Marginata'

GRASSES THAT ARE SENSITIVE TO UNDRAINED SOIL IN THE WINTER
Grasses that originate from warmer regions are often very sensitive to undrained soil in the winter. When the lower level of the ground is frozen, pools form on the ground surface from the melting snow. This standing water can cause the roots of many plants to rot. The following list of grasses are especially sensitive to rotting in winter due to too much moisture and should be planted in well-drained soil.
Arundinaria pumila
Arundinaria pygmaea
Carex buchananii
Cortaderia selloana

GRASSES THAT REQUIRE WINTER PROTECTION
Grasses originating from warm regions very often need some sort of protection during severe winters. This is done by mulching around the clump base of the grass with a dry mulch such as oak leaves or salt hay. Tender bamboo is best protected by putting the mulch into the clump between the stalks. To protect the grass from the wind, build a screen out of lumber and burlap.
Arundinaria pumila
Arundinaria pygmaea
Arundo donax
Carex buchananii
Carex morrowii 'Aurea Variegata'
Cortaderia selloana
Miscanthus sinensis 'Gracillimus'
Miscanthus sinensis 'Zebrinus'
Sinarundinaria nitida

GRASSES THAT CAN TAKE ROOT COMPETITION FROM TREES AND SHRUBS

Arundinaria pumila
Arundinaria pygmaea
Calamagrostis x acutiflora 'Stricta'
Carex morrowii 'Aurea Variegata'
Carex plantaginea
Deschampsia caespitosa and cultivars
Elymus arenarius
Molinia caerulea and cultivars

GRASSES THAT LIKE ALKALINE SOIL

Achnatherum calamagrostis
Koeleria macrantha
Melica ciliata
Sesleria autumnalis

GRASSES THAT LIKE ACIDIC SOIL

Bouteloua gracilis
Calamagrostis x acutiflora 'Stricta'
Carex grayi
Carex morrowii 'Aurea Variegata'
Carex plantaginea
Deschampsia caespitosa and cultivars
Festuca amethystina
Juncus effusus 'Spiralis'
Luzula sylvatica
Molinia caerulea and cultivars

SOURCES

Any quality nursery should be able to order ornamental grasses for you, although the majority do not carry a wide range of them as part of their regular stock. A few, however, do offer a good selection, in particular those listed below.

Bressingham Gardens
Diss, Norfolk

Country Park Nursery
Hornchurch, Essex

Greenbank Nursery
Sedbergh, Cumbria LA10 5AG

Hilliers Nurseries
Winchester, Hampshire

Jungle Giants Ltd
Morton, Bourne,
Lincolnshire PE10 0NW

Royal Horticultural Society Garden
Wisely, Ripley
Woking, Surrey CU23 6QB

Southcombe Nursery
Bickington
Newton Abbot, Devon

White Barn House
Elmstead Market
Colchester, Essex

INDEX

Page numbers in italics refer to captions, illustrations, and sidebars.

A

Achnatherum calamagrostis, 34-35, 90
Acidic soil grasses, 121
Acorus sp., 18
Agricultural grasses, 21
Alkaline soil grasses, 121
American Beach Grass. *See Ammophilia breviligulata*
Amethyst Blue Fescue. *See Festuca amethystina*
Ammophilia breviligulata, 80, 90
Andropogon scoparius, 43, 90
Annuals, grasses combined with, 47
Arrhenatherum elatius bulbosum, 41, 91
Arrow grass. *See Triglochin* sp.
Arundinaria, 65
Arundinaria nitada, 38, 93
Arundinaria pygmaea, 41, 92
Arundinaria sp., 22
Arundinaria viridi-striata, 92
Arundo donax, 38, 93
Asia (middle), 21
Asters, 65
Astilbe chinensis, 85
Astilboides tabularis, 38

Australian Fountain Grass. *See Pennistum alopecuroides*
Autumnal grasses, 120
Autumn Moor Grass. *See Sesleria autumnalis*

B

Bamboo, 22, *29,* 31, 65, *69,* 92, 93
    containment of, 42-43
    height of, 26
Bambusa sp., 22
Beach Grass. *See Elymus* sp.
Beach grasses, 31
Bible, bulrushes mentioned in, 18
Big Quaking Grass. *See Briza maxima*
Black-eyed Susans. *See Rudbeckia*
Blue Fescue. *See Festuca ovina*
Blue foliage, grasses with, 120
Blue Lyme Grass. *See Elymus arenarius*
Blue Oat Grass. *See Helictotrichon sempervirens*
Blue shrub. *See Caryopteris*
Bogs, grasses for, 38, 119
Borders, ornamental grasses for, *34-35*
Bottlebrush Grass. *See Hystrix patula*
Bouteloua gracilis, 94
Bouteloua sp., 43
Bracts, 14
Briza maxima, 43, 94

Briza media, 94
Broad-leaved Meadow Grass. *See Poa chaixii*
Bulbous Oat Grass. *See Arrhenatherum elatius bulbosum*
Bulrushes, 18

C

Calamagrostis acutiflora, 30, 95
Canna sp., 86
Carex buchananii, 95
Carex conica, 21
Carex grayi, 21, 96
Carex morrowii, 21, 96
Carex muskingumensis, 97
Carex pendula, 21
Carex plantaginea, 21, 97
Carex sp., *13,* 21, *29,* 31, 33-34, 41, 43
    propagation of, *42-43*
Caryopsis, in Gramineae family, 14
Caryopteris, 86
Cattails. *See* Typhaceae family
Chasmanthium latifolium. See Uniola latifolia
Chimonobambusa sp., 22
Chinese Silver Grass. *See Miscanthus sinensis*
Coastal gardens, ornamental grasses for, 37-38
Common Rush. *See Juncus effusus*
Comprehensive designs, 77-87

Cord Grass. *See Spartina pectinata*
Cortaderia selloana, 29, 70, 98
Cotyledon, 14
Crested Hair Grass. *See Koeleria macrantha*
Crimson Fountain Grass. *See Pennisetum setaceum*
Culms, definition and characteristics of, 17
Cymbopogon citratus, 98
Cyperaceae family, *16-17,* 17-18
   Carex sp. within, *13*
   definition and characteristics of, 17
   number of genera in, 17
Cyperus esculentus, 18
Cyperus bydra, 14

D

Dactylis glomerata, 98
Daylilies, 75
Deschampsia caespitosa, 42, 43, 51, 65, 99
Deschampsia sp., 80
Dune grass, erosion control using, *18*
Dusty miller, 80

E

Ecology, grass' role in, 21
Elymus arenarius, 37, 80, 100
Elymus sp., *20,* 38
Eragrostis trichodes, 43, 100
Erianthus ravennae, 101
Erosion
   dune grass to control, *18*
   Elymus to control, *20*
   grass to control, 19
   lawn grasses and, 27
Ethiopia, 21
Eulalia Grass. *See Miscanthus sinensis*
Eupatorium purpurea, 86
European Dune Grass. *See Elymus arenarius*

Evergreen grasses, 120
Evergreens, grasses combined with, 51

F

Featherpoppy. *See Macleaya cordata*
Feather Reed Grass. *See Calamagrostis acutiflora*
Feather Top. *See Pennisetum villosum*
Ferns, 75
Fescue. *See Festuca* sp.
Festuca amethystina, 101
Festuca mairei, 43, 102
Festuca ovina, 27, *28, 29,* 101
   as ground cover, 28
Festuca sp., 14, 33-34, 37-38, 41, 47, 55
Fixed structural elements, 56-68
Flowers
   to border walkways, 63
   of Cyperaceae family, 17
   inflorescence and, 14
   in Juncaceae family, 16
Fountain Bamboo. *See Arundinaria nitida*
Fountain Grass. *See Pennisetum setaceum*
Fox-tail Barley. *See Hordeum jubatum*
Fruit
   grass and rush compared, 16
   See also Caryopsis

G

Gardener's Garters. *See Phalaris arundinacea*
Gardens
   ornamental grasses in, 33
   See also specific types of gardens
Germination
   in Gramineae family, 14
   See also Seeds
Giant Chinese Silver Grass. *See Miscanthus floridulus*
Giant Reed. *See Arundo donax*

Glyceria maxima, 102
Gramineae family, 14-15
   caryopsis in, 14
   characteristics of, 14
   number of species within, 14
   spikelet arrangement in, 14, *15*
Grasses
   ecological role of, 21
   erosion control using, *20*
   as ground cover, 27, 28, *33,* 33-34, 118
   misconceptions concerning, 12
   natural habitat of, 19-21
   ornamental types, *29*
   planting distance, 41
   rhizomatous invaders, *40-41*
   running-rhizome varieties, 27-28
   rush fruit compared with, 16
   seasonal stability of, 31, 42
   society and, 22
   specimen plantings, 118
   tufted-species, 27
   water and height of, 71
Gray's Sedge. *See Carex grayi*
Greater Wood Rush. *See Luzula sylvatica*
Ground covers, grasses as, 27, 28, *33,* 33-34, 118

H

Hakonechloa macra, 103
Helictotrichon sempervirens, 43, 75, 79, 103
Heliopsis sp., 48
Hibiscus, 86
Holcus mollis, 104
Hordeum jubatum, 43, 104
Hosta sp., 38, 75, 86
Houses, *Molinia* in front of, 62
Humus, *18-19*
   grass conversion to, 19
Hystrix patula, 43, 105

I

Imperata cylindrica, 40-41, 105
Inflorescence, 14, *15*, 17
Iran, 21
Iris cristata, 18
Iris kaempferi, 86
Ivy, 65

J

Japanese Blood Grass. *See Imperata cylindrica*
Japanese gardens, 69
Japanese iris. *See Iris kaempferi*
Japanese Sedge Grass. *See Carex morrowii*
Joe-pye weed. *See Eupatorium purpurea*
Juncaceae family, 16
Juncus effusus, 22, 43, 106

K

Koeleria macrantha, 106

L

Lake grasses, 21
Lawns, *26*, 26-27
Leatherleaf Sedge Grass. *See Carex buchananii*
Leaves
    cotyledon, 14
    in Juncaceae family, 16
    as most recognizable characteristic, 14
Lemon Grass. *See Cymbopogon citratus*
Ligularia sp., 38
Little Blue Stem. *See Andropogon scoparius*
Luzula nivea, 41
Luzula sp., 33-34, 43
Luzula sylvatica, 41, 107

M

Macleaya cordata, 86
Maiden Grass. *See Miscanthus sinensis*
Maires Fescue. *See Festuca mairei*
Marshmallow. *See Hibiscus*
Melica ciliata, 107
Miscanthus floridulus, 51, 107
Miscanthus sacchariflorus, 109
Miscanthus sinensis, *29*, 47, 51, 62, 63, 71-73, 75, 86, 109, 110, 111
Miscanthus sp., 14, *30*, 38, 53
    as accent plant, 31
Moisture, retention in grass of, 19, *20*
Molinia caerulea, 75, 79, 113
Molinia sp., 43, 62
Moor Grass. *See Molinia caerulea*
Mosquito Grass. *See Bouteloua gracilis*
Mound-forming grasses, 119
Mountain grasses, 21
Mountains, humus produced on, *18-19*
Mulching, 41-42

N

Natural gardens, 118
    ornamental grasses for, 34-36
Northern Sea Oats. *See Uniola latifolia*
Nut Grass. *See Cyperus esculentus*; *Cyperus hydra*

O

Oriental Fountain Grass. *See Pennisetum orientale*

P

Palm Branch Sedge, *16-17*. *See Carex muskingumensis*
Pamir Mountains, 21
Pampas Grass. *See Cortaderia selloana*
Panicle arrangement, 14, *15*

P

Panicum sp., 14, 38
Panicum virgatum, *30*, 31, 113
Papyrus, 22
Pendulous weeping shapes, grasses with, 119
Pennisetum alopecuroides, *12-13*, *20*, *29*, 51, 59-61, 113
Pennisetum orientale, 43, 113
Pennisetum setaceum, *34-35*, 43, 47, 114
Pennisetum sp., 14, 80
Pennisetum villosum, 114
Perennial borders, grasses for, 38, 119
Perennial gardens, *32-33*
Phalaris arundinacea, *26-27*, 27, *29*, 51, 61, 86, 115
    for perennial borders, *38-39*
    as rhizomatous invader, *41*
Phalaris arundinaria, 48
Phalaris sp., 38
Phragmites australis, 21, 38
Phyllostachys aurea, *69*
Phyllostachys aureosulcata, *93*
Phyllostachys sp., 22, *42*
Picta. *See Phalaris arundinacea*
Planting distance, 41
Poa chaixii, 43, 116
Polygonum sp., 86
Pond grasses, 21
Ponds
    grasses for edge of, 38, 119
    natural settings for, 71
Pools, ornamental grasses for, *57*, 75-76
Porcupine Grass. *See Miscanthus sinensis*
Pseudosasa sp., 22
Purple Moor Grass. *See Molinia caerulea*
Pygmy Bamboo. *See Arundinaria*

Q

Quaking Grass. *See Briza media*

R

Raceme arrangement, 14, *15*
Ravenna Grass. *See Erianthus ravennae*
Red foliage, grasses with, 120
Red Switch Grass. *See Panicum*
Reed Sweet Grass. *See Glyceria maxima*
Ribbon Grass. *See Phalaris arundinacea*
River grasses, 21
Rock gardens, 118
   ornamental grasses for, 34
Rodgersia sp., 38
Root competition, *36*, 121
Rudbeckia sp., 47, 71-73, 86
Rushes. *See* Juncaceae family
Rush wheat. *See Triticum junceum*

S

Sand Love Grass. *See Eragrostis trichodes*
Sasa sp., 22
Schizaachyrium scoparium. See Andropogon scoparius
Scirpus lacustris, 18
Screens, grasses as, 26
Seashore gardens, 119
Sedge Grass, *16-17*
Sedum sp., 47, 71-73, 86
Seeds
   in Gramineae family, 14
   grasses propagated by, 43
Sepals, as characteristic of Juncaceae, 16
Sesleria autumnalis, 116
Sesleria sp., 41
Shade, *36*
Shallow water, grasses for, 38, 119
Shibataea sp., 22
Shrubs
   root competition with, 121
   vertical elements of, 55

Silky-Spike Melic Grass. *See Melica ciliata*
Silver Banner Grass. *See Miscanthus sacchariflorus*
Silverfeather Grass. *See Miscanthus sinensis*
Silver Spike Grass. *See Achnatherum calamagrostis*
Sinarundinaria nitida. See Arundinaria nitada
Sinarundinaria sp., 22, 41
Soft Rush. *See Juncus effusus*
Spartina pectinata, 38, 116
Specimens, ornamental grasses as, 34, 118
Spike arrangement, 14, *15*
Spikelets, 14, *15*
Spodiopogon sibiricus, 116
Spreading grasses, 120
Stems
   basal meristems, 27, 28
   of Cyperaceae family, 17
Stipa sp., 41, 43
Stone paths, 79-80
Streams, grasses for borders of, 85
Striped Eulalia Grass. *See Miscanthus sinensis*
Structural elements, 56-68
Swamp Foxtail Grass. *See Pennisetum alopecuroides*
Switch Grass. *See Panicum* sp.; *Panicum virgatum*

T

Topsoil, 41
Trees
   root competition with, 121
   vertical elements of, 55
Triglochin sp., 18
Triticum junceum, 17-18
Tufted Hair Grass. *See Deschampsia caespitosa*
Typhaceae family, 18
Typha latifolia, 18

U

Uniola latifolia, 43, 117

V

Variegated Cocksfoot. *See Dactylis glomerata*
Variegated Creeping Soft Grass. *See Holcus mollis*
Variegation, grasses with, 119-20
Vertical lines, grasses with, 119
Vitex sp., 86

W

Walkways
   borders for, 63-65
   ornamental grasses for, *34-35*
   ornamental grasses to soften edges of, *56-57*
   stone path, 79-80
Water
   ornamental grasses and, 69-76
   See also Ponds; Shallow water
Weeds, 41-42
Wheat, *22-23*
Wide Leaf Sedge. *See Carex plantaginea*
Wild gardens, 118
   ornamental grasses for, 34-36
Winter, grasses unsuitable for, 120
Wintergreen grasses, 120
Woodland gardens, 118
   ornamental grasses for, 36-37
Woodland grasses, 21

Y

Yellow Groove Bamboo. *See Phyllostachys aurea*
Yucca, 75

Z

Zebra Grass. *See Miscanthus sinensis*
Zinnias, grass combined with, 47